'The funniest frog in print' *Daily Mail*

'Opinionated, French and severely witty [Poirier] writes beautiful, clear, neatly measured English, embroidered with flourishes of vernacular . . . Lively, sardonic, always poised, the book strikes impressive moments of balance' *Scotsman*

'Perhaps the most fascinating thing about this book is . . . what it tells us about France' *Spectator*

'Perhaps it doesn't sound like much fun to be set straight on everything . . . by a French "intellectual" . . . Strangely, it is'
Daily Telegraph

'Politics, society, food, art . . . are all discussed with a cheerful wit, backed up by . . . more serious historical and philosophical observations' *New Statesman*

'Funny and fascinating bid to uncover the differences between us Brits and the French . . . full of side-splitting observations about our various attitudes, customs and traditions' *OK*

Writer and broadcaster Agnès Catherine Poirier is primarily a political journalist and film critic for *Libération*, *Télérama* and a regular commentator for the *Guardian* and the BBC.

Touché

AGNÈS CATHERINE POIRIER

PHOENIX

A PHOENIX PAPERBACK

First published in Great Britain in 2006
by Weidenfeld & Nicolson
This paperback edition published in 2007
by Phoenix,
an imprint of Orion Books Ltd,
Orion House, 5 Upper St Martin's Lane,
London WC2H 9EA

An Hachette Livre UK company

3 5 7 9 10 8 6 4 2

A CIP catalogue record for this book
is available from the British Library.

ISBN 978-0-7538-2170-1

Typeset at The Spartan Press Ltd,
Lymington, Hants

Printed and bound in Great Britain at Mackays of Chatham plc,
Chatham, Kent

The Orion Publishing Group's policy is to use papers that
are natural, renewable and recyclable products and
made from wood grown in sustainable forests. The logging
and manufacturing processes are expected to conform to
the environmental regulations of the country of origin.

www.orionbooks.co.uk

Au père!

Contents

'Wickedness is a myth invented by good people
to account for the curious attractiveness of others.'

Oscar Wilde

Preface

British friends, never doubt the admiration you inspire.

I was twenty-three when I came to live in London, and for me there was nothing Britain or the British could do wrong: they were perfect to a fault. I was *bien-sûr* a raging Anglophile. Where did my Anglomania come from? First of all, from Voltaire. He must have had good reason to think Britain was marvellous, I thought. There was also the enigmatic smile of a dashing young man whom I never met but whose black-and-white photograph welcomed all visitors to my Great-aunt Marie's house until her death in 1991. This young man was Tonton Keith, her beloved husband, who died tragically young in 1947.

As a history student, I was overwhelmed by the tales of Londoners' heroism during the Blitz, especially when, at the same time, I had to deal with the dangerous apathy most of my compatriots had shown during the war. Didn't I owe my freedom to young men from Britain, America and Canada, many of whom sacrificed their youth and never returned from the beaches of Normandy? My mother certainly did; she was eight then, and, to this day, *la Libération* has remained the most beautiful day of her life.

Shakespeare, in the amazing translations by French poet Yves Bonnefoy, proved to be a revelation in my adolescent years. So did Conan Doyle. My two elder brothers weren't fanatical about Britain; they chose Spain as their favourite linguistic destination. However, there was one thing English my brother Janot had no reservations about: Maltesers. He was the high priest of that faith, and I became a fervent disciple. I also drank tea by the gallon, like my Great-aunt Marie, and I loved shortbread.

Romance-wise, at a very early age I had fallen for the mellifluous voices of British legends such as James Mason, George Sanders and Dirk Bogarde. Then, at the age of seventeen, I went to see *Valmont* by Milos Forman, a forgotten masterpiece with Colin Firth in the leading role . . .

Next came politics.

In January 1995, I told everybody and also managed to convince myself that 'If Chirac is ever president, I'll flee to London like de Gaulle did in 1940.' When I saw Jacques's face appear on my TV screen at 8 p.m. sharp on 7 May, I knew my fate was sealed. In truth, I had applied to do a degree at a London university, and I had already been accepted. But I did partly believe that bit of pretentious nonsense about Chirac making me take flight to London. When Chirac was elected again, this time with my vote, in 2002, my friends teased me: 'So, another five years in London, then?' They have recently looked increasingly worried: 'In 2007, if Sarkozy's elected, you're taking up arms, aren't you?' I might, actually. Or I like to think I would.

So, on the afternoon of 28 September 1995, I bought a single ticket to London. My father drove me to Gare du Nord and walked me to the check-in gate. The Hundred Years War didn't feel so far away: I was defecting to the old enemy, I could see it in his eyes. I travelled on the Eurostar for the first time, wearing black jodhpur trousers, a white shirt and a black jacket. I had come to England to become English, in a radical, all-or-nothing French way.

However, I'm more French today than I ever was: I mean, I'm so acutely aware of the French as seen by the British that I can play hide-and-seek with national stereotypes and prejudices. I constantly observe my compatriots and myself through the eyes of foreigners, and what I see is not always flattering. I go back to France and observe this strange species: the French. In Britain, I observe another very exotic type: the British.

*

Touché is the fruit of an Anglo-Saxon conspiracy. Let me explain. In 2005, I published my first book in French, *Les Nouveaux Anglais*, a light essay (with an unashamedly French perspective) on the English today, a book written by a French person for a French readership. British press correspondents in Paris read the book before it even hit the bookshops and wrote headlines[1] such that I found myself in no time sitting next to Richard and Judy on Channel 4. The British publicity didn't do much for the book, as, alas, nobody reads French any more in Britain, but the media brouhaha surrounding it certainly made me realise how sensitive the English could be about themselves, especially if seen by a French citizen. Tabloids attacked me for mocking the Queen – how dare I? – and for criticising, even slightly, my best friends. I tried to explain that there is no love without teasing, but my attempts at *déclaration d'amour pour les Anglais* seemed to fall on deaf ears.

When the wonderful Alan Samson from Weidenfeld and Nicolson acquired the UK rights for *Les Nouveaux Anglais*, I knew there would be some work to do once the translation was complete. When our translator, the superb Polly McLean, gave us her version, I could but marvel at her shrewd eye and razor-sharp skills; I also realised, however, that *Les Nouveaux Anglais* would drown somewhere off the shore of Dover, just like one of those Italian or German comedies: successful at home but impossible to export.

I'm for ever grateful to Alan Samson and Polly McLean for having enabled me to write a whole new book, in the English language, for an English readership.

---

1. Among them: 'French book casts Britons as un-erotic binge drinkers', the *Daily Telegraph*, 11 April 2005; 'You un-erotic, pet-obsessed binge drinkers', the *Daily Mail*, 12 April 2005; 'You crazy Rosbifs', the *Guardian*, 12 April 2005.

I would also like to thank François Ivernel for his *infatigable* support and diplomatic advice, Henri-Louis Poirier for his enlightened opinion and Buzz Baum for his constructive critique. I particularly thank François for his: 'You arrogant French swine, there are things you cannot say about the English. It's not simply because it is true that you can write it.' I thank Henri for his: 'Hmm, you're right, the English are really not like us,' and Buzz for his: 'The writing is so intense I often gasped for air.'

Finally, I thank Alison Mann for her peerless and lightning-speed proof-reading.

This book is dedicated to my father, who, for the last ten years of his life, each time I'd kiss him goodbye would wink and say, 'So, you're going back to your *île du diable*? *Reviens vite!*'

1

Act!

'Britain's youth want to save whales, but it is hard to imagine them renouncing the wares of Sony and Sanyo in the cause, as the Hains renounced apartheid sherry. They are dismayed by horrors in Africa, but would rather spend Saturday afternoon watching Man U than demonstrating outside Downing Street about Western supineness.'[1] Max Hastings

'What can a poor boy do, except sing for a rock 'n' roll band, 'cause in sleepy London town, there's just no place for a street-fighting man.' Rolling Stones

Right, I'm a French citizen and I'm angry with the government for one reason or another. What do I do? Theoretically, I have a wide range of options for action, just like the average English citizen: I can draw up and sign a petition; I can contact my local MP; I can set up a blog; I can vote; boycott; lobby; or shout in my bathroom. I can do all sorts of things, but somehow the first action that springs to mind is 'Take to the streets!'.

And I'm not alone, as *manifester*, or demonstrating, is to this day the way we express dissent in France. There has, however,

1. Quoted in the *Guardian*, 27 April 2005.

always been a divide between the people on the Right and the people on the Left, who are far more prone to street action. There are entire families in France who have never taken part in a demonstration – out of fear, snobbery and contempt for those on the Left who dare rebel. But these are few in number. And on exceptional occasions, even the Right take to the streets. On 30 May 1968, a million French people marched in Paris to show their solidarity with General de Gaulle in his fight against the May 1968 student rioters and strikers. On 24 June 1984, another million French (surely the same population as in 1968) marched to fight for *l'école libre* – i.e. half-state, half-private schools. As a dear friend of mine, brought up in one of these right-wing families, once said to me, 'Some people prefer to demonstrate *for* rather than *against* . . .'

In Paris, the idea of demonstrating is even more sacred than anywhere else in the country, as building barricades was a recurrent feature in the capital's history from the French Revolution up to 1968. Yet, now that a layer of tarmac has covered the cobblestoned streets, one has to make do with peaceful demonstrations. But give Parisians a good reason and they might just find another way to reclaim their glorious past . . . Never forget that each time we demonstrate we're re-enacting the fall of the Bastille, no less. We may not be aware of it, but that's the tune we're playing with our feet each time we take to the streets.

As long as there are people to organise *manifs*,[2] we'll be there. It's always seemed so simple. Putin is in town to visit his pal Jacques; somehow it annoys you. Before you can even think about what you could do to show your disapproval, the news on the radio tells you that there will be a *manif* tomorrow in place du Panthéon from 5 p.m. Easy, all you have to do is turn up. There may end up being only a few hundred of you, but it doesn't really matter. You will have raised your voice, shouted a

2. *Petit nom* of *manifestation*, i.e. demonstration.

few slogans and listened to your favourite intellectual speak of how Putin is the cruellest tsar Russia has ever known.[3] Now that you've vented your anger you feel fine, energised, like after a jog in the park. Demonstrating feels good, as healthy as going to the shrink, and, what's more, it's free.

That's it, that's how it is: something in the news really upsets you? Rest assured there will be a *manif* to attend somewhere in France, and most likely in Paris. I'm thirty-three and cannot even recall how many demonstrations I have been to, and I'm far from being as active a demonstrator as some of my friends, who as we say in French, demonstrate like they breathe. I remember as a student taking the Eurostar to go back home and demonstrate in the streets of Paris. That's what cheap student fares are for, aren't they?

I remember the first time that I marched. A first demonstration is like a first kiss – for ever imprinted on one's mind – except, in my case, demonstrating was even better than a *coup de foudre*.[4] It was December 1986 and I was fourteen. Alain Devaquet was the Conservative education minister whose new law incensed French students.[5] Honestly, I hadn't read the law and was not even affected by it as a *lycéenne*, and therefore still at school, but it was the first opportunity for me and my classmates to take to the streets like our elders and, at last, to pass the French citizens' test of revolt. Plus it was a chance to fight riot police, the famous CRS, or at the very least to call them names like 'CRS-SS'! It all sounds ludicrously romantic, and it was. But we would soon realise that it was also damned serious.

---

3. Ever wondered why France doesn't boast any decent rock stars? Because our own rock stars are our intellectuals, and some of them are rather beautiful stallions; I mean they have very attractive minds. No need for Mick Jagger when we have Alain Finkielkraut. I'm serious.
4. Love at first sight (as if hit by lightning).
5. In a nutshell, Devaquet planned to introduce higher fees and more selection in French universities.

We marched on 4 and 6 December in freezing-cold Paris. On 8 December, Devaquet resigned and his law was scrapped. One student had died, beaten up by riot police in rue Monsieur le Prince just next to the Sorbonne. His name was Malik Oussekine.

Since 1986, there have been many more *manifs* – up to ten every week: tiny ones and huge ones, from 2,000 demonstrators to over a million. In Paris, they usually take the route of place de la République to Nation via La Bastille. Sometimes the turnover of *manifs* is crazy, such as between 21 April 2002, when Le Pen found himself in the second round of the presidential election opposing Chirac, and 5 May, when Chirac was elected with 80% of the vote. For two weeks, 1 to 2 million people demonstrated every day throughout France. Hey, you don't often have to choose between a staunch right-winger and a Right extremist for future president! Only in France . . .

By the way, demonstrations are not the only way to express anger in France, even if they are, by far, our favourite. Striking and *opérations coup de poing*[6] are also a must, as reported for instance by the *Guardian*:

> When it comes to protests, nobody does it better than the French – witness the police demonstrations against crime. But when direct action is called for, the French are also peerless. After reporting on the disgruntled Gallic wine-makers who shot up tankers carrying 'foreign plonk' from neighbouring Spain, *Le Journal du Dimanche* turned its attention to the angry fruit farmers from south-west France who carried out 'commando operations' on discount supermarkets, which they blame for falling profits. One hundred or so tractors invaded the parking area of a dozen supermarkets in Perpignan. At each stage, 300 farmers dumped 20 tonnes of fruit and vegetables.

---

6. Loosely translated as a 'fist in your face operations'.

And the protesters' *coup de grâce*? They appropriated the supermarket trolleys and threw them in the river.[7]

So I arrive in the UK in 1995 and what do I find? A great country in which almost nothing works, or not as well as it used to, and not as well as it does elsewhere. I hear for the first time in my life the most preposterous excuses for hours of delay in the tube or on the rail network: 'The train service has stopped because of the heavy rain' or ' . . . because of leaves on the tracks'. I look around in disbelief; nobody stirs, nobody sighs, and nobody even raises an eyebrow. Incredible, *incroyable*! The English can take everything. Nothing seems to make them angry. They never complain out loud like my fellow country-men. Admirable. And absolutely infuriating. When will they take to the streets to vent their anger? When will they find a situation untenable? Never – well, almost.

In the ten years I've lived in London, the British have taken to the streets twice, and these were the biggest demonstrations in contemporary British history. Four hundred thousand Brits demonstrated against . . . the ban on fox-hunting on 22 September 2002,[8] and then, breaking all records, a million people demonstrated against the war in Iraq on 15 February 2003. I'm glad I was here. Now at least I know they can do it.

I have tried to understand the fundamental difference between collective action in the UK and in France. There are many reasons, but one is clear: although England gave shelter to Karl, Marxism never influenced the British the way it affected and shaped our way of thinking in France. Even among the Fabians – the intellectual theorists of the Labour movement from the 1880s onward – Marxism and its confrontational views were never popular. Fabians – British socialists – were reformists not revolutionaries. They were rationalists, utilitarians; they thought

7. Kim Willsher, the *Guardian*, 22 July 2005.
8. Against a ban on fox-hunting . . . The British must be bonkers.

that what men had to do above all was to behave sensibly, rather than break dramatically with the past. Fabians never considered class struggle to be an instrument of change. Maybe they weren't even aware of it as a possibility! They also weren't the slightest bit interested in confronting non-socialists or anybody who didn't share their views. Just think of the origin of their name: Fabianism is named after Quintus Fabius Maximus Cunctator, known as 'the Delayer', a Roman general who advocated harassment and attrition tactics rather than head-on battles against the Carthaginian army and General Hannibal. When you know that Labour is a loose reincarnation of Fabianism, you cannot fail to understand that violent street confrontation could never be a natural way for the English Left to express themselves, let alone the Liberals or Conservatives.

In France, it was almost totally the opposite. Marxism and Socialism were one, and still are today in so many ways. Of course, there were always reformists, partisans of democratic Socialism such as Ledru-Rollin and Louis Blanc (who both got a Métro station named after them). However, they were outnumbered by the advocates of violent action. By those such as Robespierre, Barbès and Blanqui. (The first two got a Métro station, the other a boulevard.) Deeply rooted in France's national psyche is the belief that it can only evolve and reform its economic and social system through episodes of extreme violence. Look at Jean Jaurès. (Yeah, he got a Métro station too.) This emblematic figure of the French Left had one ambition: marry *la République* to socialism, marry Marxism with liberal ideas from the French Revolution, and patriotism with internationalism. Even in December 1920, when the French Left divided to give birth to the revolutionary Communist Party on the one hand and to the Democratic Socialist SFIO on the other,[9] the latter remained

---

9. Section Française de l'Internationale Ouvrière, the ancestor of the Socialist Party.

Marxist in spirit. Remember that Mitterrand when elected in 1981, governed with French communists. Today, the Parti Socialiste is still permeated with Marxism. They don't seem to have noticed that the Western world has entered a post-materialist age.

To sum up, the French believe in confrontation and the English don't, and this doesn't only apply to taking to the streets. Example: on 21 November 2005, the journalists of the daily newspaper *Libération* decide to go on strike. The management is asking for fifty-two people to go, but, for the first time in the newspaper's history, the redundancies are not on a voluntary basis. The journalists simply won't accept it. For four days, the newspaper is not written, not printed, and is absent from news-stands. The journalists risk losing everything, but they don't care. And in the end they get what they want: a big fat cheque *if and when* they decide to leave. Only in France. Is this admirable? I'm not so sure. But such a situation is beyond the wildest imaginings of any British journalist. Whenever British journalists go on strike, they actually take pride in publishing some kind of edition, so that the readership doesn't lose its habit of buying. They would never dream of not printing an issue of the paper, even on strike.

One last revealing thing about France: this is a country where Arlette Laguiller, leader of the party Force Ouvrière, won a big accolade from the French in a recent poll about politicians – 50% of them (and 65% of the people on the Left) say they like her, making her one of the five most popular politicians in the country.[10] I should mention that Arlette Laguiller is a Trotskyite who advocates international Bolshevik revolution and proletariat dictatorship in France. So what does this say about French politics? Certainly that many French people have become radicalized in their views. They long for a time when conflicts will once again be clearly defined: workers vs. capitalist pigs.

10. An IPSOS poll, 22 August 2001.

The complexity of our global world seems to frighten them more than they'd like to admit.

It's true, the English are nostalgic too: nostalgic for the protests of the Swinging Sixties. Some like their nostalgia light! Columnist and satirical writer Craig Brown writes about the sixties 'protest culture' in his his classically British self-deprecating way:

> The sixties witnessed an increasing amount of student rest, often involving lengthy sit-ins. Young people would sit down, often on top of one another. It was all part of what was termed the Generation Lap. Other notable demonstrations of the time included cookery, yoga, origami and dental meditation. Demonstrations were more idealistic in America, and more glamorous in France, but at least in Britain they were much less crowded. Whereas the American protest movement took as its slogan 'Tune In, Turn Over and Drop Out', the British protest movement preferred the more relaxing 'Tune In, Turn Over and Drop Off'.[11]

However, some English commentators are less than happy with this nostalgia-light. In an article called 'Bring back rent-a-mob', commentator Max Hastings complains about today's students:

> Even if a minority are working harder than we ever did, most still have plenty of leisure. They simply choose to spend it in different ways. They would rather drink than demonstrate. They are more passionate about sport than the fate of Iraq. It seems bizarre to be promoting the cause of student activism. Yet surely anyone who cares about British democracy should be bothered about our culture of acquiescence, not least in the re-election of a British prime minister who committed the

11. Craig Brown, *1966 and All That* (Hodder & Stoughton, 2005).

nation to war on the basis of massive falsehoods, some of George Bush's making but most of his own.

The young are supposed to cherish vain hopes and go to the barricades for foolish causes. A world in which a college dean protests while his students swot in their rooms or head for the pub is topsy-turvy indeed. Bring back rent-a-mob. It does not matter what they protest about, if they will only bestir themselves to become agitated about something.[12]

Perhaps the English don't protest as much as their elders because they are afraid of doing so. On 1 August 2005, a new law banned protests from within half a mile of the House of Commons that do not have advance permission from the Metropolitan Police. On 28 September 2005, a veteran Labour delegate and Jewish refugee from the Nazis, Walter Wolfgang, age eighty-two, was man-handled and ejected from the Labour Party conference hall for heckling the government about its policy on the war in Iraq. He was then refused readmission under the Prevention of Terrorism Act. On 3 October 2005, six students from Lancaster University appealed against their convictions: they had been prosecuted and found guilty of disrupting a corporate event at their university. In fact, they had staged a five-minute peaceful demonstration on campus.

Considering that the sacrosanct French right to demonstrate can be translated in the British political culture into the right of free speech, one really wonders why current legislation in the UK attempts to criminalise one of the greatest British traditions. One can't put it all down to the London bombings of 7 July 2005. Why would one wish to gag protesters when all they do is criticise the shortcomings of the Blair government? Surely British judges can distinguish between them and the fundamentalist lunatics who call for murder.

12. Comments pages of the *Guardian*, 27 April 2005.

Even the trade unions are no longer a refuge for British dissenters. Thatcher managed to strip them of most of their rights. They have stopped being a counterpoint to corporate power. Of course, you still hear them from time to time, but their voice is faint. Remember Gate Gourmet in August 2005? When I had to explain to French readers that going on strike out of solidarity for fellow workers was illegal in the UK,[13] I was met with bewilderment. Surely I must be kidding? In France, fewer and fewer people are members of trade unions, but there remain some strongholds, notably within state industries such as the railways. As a result, French society is divided in two: one half that is badly represented, and the other that is refusing to give even an inch of their *avantages acquis*, or benefits. The latter lives in a dream-world of ten weeks' paid holiday, retirement at fifty-five and so forth. How long for? Who knows? As long as the majority of French people support their action, they can get away with murder.

Despite all their differences, Britain and France now both suffer from similar collective-action ills. In both countries, the younger generation seems reluctant to engage in 'traditional' politics, as we know it. Today, many refuse to identify with a political party and prefer to militate for 'bigger' issues such as poverty in the world or environmental problems. A recent poll in France has shown that only 30% of teenagers accept the concept of Left and Right (as opposed to 82% of adults); 78% of French teenagers admit to not talking much about politics with friends or at home, yet 45% have taken part in a demonstration.[14] What they are drawn to, it seems, is protest in the abstract, in a vacuum, rather than politics. And whom do they worship? Bono and Geldof.

Indeed, today, we've left it to rock and film stars to define

13. Employment Act 1990.
14. An IPSOS poll, February 2001.

protest culture. Bob Dylan's songs can still be heard in marches in the US or in the UK, *faute de mieux*. George Clooney in his film about Ed Murrow,[15] *Good Night, and Good Luck*, tells us of a time when a major US television network would risk all to fight for a principle.

Writer Ian Buruma sums up the spirit of today's protest culture eloquently:

> The very idea of Dylan going to the White House, or World Summit meetings, to discuss the fate of the world is ridiculous. Yet this is precisely what most political rock stars of today are doing: accepting medals, having meetings with presidents and prime ministers, receiving knighthoods. What is a rock 'n' roller like Bono doing when he gives out official statements from the G8 Summit praising George Bush for his generosity to Africa? And what about those 'signed copies' of Bob Geldof's photographs taken during his African journeys? This is politics too, of a kind, but it is not exactly fizzing with protest against the established order.[16]

Take the Make Poverty History campaign: what an odd protest – it essentially gives its blessing to government policy. Looks like Blairite spin. As for its string of merchandising, it definitely looks as if today's protest has turned into another capitalist enterprise. Exactly like rock music, whose 1970s independent labels were bought by big companies. Those companies then merged into gigantic media conglomerates in the 1980s. Protest rock songs of the past are now used to promote *tout et n'importe quoi*, everything and anything: sportswear or politics. Angela Merkel chose the Stones' 'Angie' as her campaign song . . .

15. An American journalist who took on senator Joseph McCarthy's anti-communist witch-hunt in 1954 through his news programme *See It Now*.
16. Ian Buruma, the *Guardian*, 12 November 2005.

In our post-materialist and post-Marxist Western world, new social conflicts are on the rise that are barely organised and which seem to be made for the media itself. The protesters tend to be uneducated, dissatisfied youth with little grasp of democracy. Some of them even question the very democratic values that define our Western world. This pernicious *ménage à trois* of disaffection, poorly articulated demands and dependence on the media leaves little room for Politics. The result: mayhem. As witnessed, for instance, in France in October 2005 during the so-called French Riots. Most of it was pure nihilism born of economic and social exclusion. There were no overt political demands, just a display of anger. And a fascination for seeing empty acts of violencet played and replayed on TV. Looking at themselves in a triple-mirror, and loving every moment of it, the *sauvageons'* narcissism seemed to grow and grow.[17] These riots however were to the great satisfaction of Nicolas Sarkozy, home secretary and presidential hopeful, for, in many ways, they were the offspring of the insidious politics of laissez-faire and disengagement from the State that are favoured by free-marketeers such as Sarkozy. Nicolas washes his hands of the riots. What an unexpected blessing! If they last until the May 2007 presidential elections, terrified French voters may look to him giving Sarkozy the upper hand. One can only hope that the other half of France will resort to barricades again. What else?

Not another rock concert!

17. *Sauvageons* is an almost affectionate term used by former Interior Minister Jean-Pierre Chevènement to describe the disaffected youth of France's suburbs. Certainly a better term than 'rabble' (or *racaille*) used by current Interior Minister Nicolas Sarkozy.

2

Americans

'The absence of wine at our meals at first struck us as very disagreeable; and we still can't understand the multitude of things that they succeed in introducing into their stomachs here. You see, in addition to breakfast, dinner and tea with which the Americans eat ham, they also eat a very copious supper, and often a *goûter*. That up to now is the only indisputable superiority that I grant them over us. But they see in themselves many others. These people seem to me stinking with national conceit; it pierces through all their courtesy.' Alexis de Tocqueville on the Americans[1]

'As between the reliability of the French and the Americans as allies for this country, I cannot imagine that any citizen of the United Kingdom in his right mind has the slightest doubt about which country is more reliable, not to mention which country is of more use to us [. . .] With all due respect, what France brings to the party is essentially hot air and skulduggery.' Lord Black[2]

'The truth is that France likes glory, but only the glory

1. In a letter to his mother written on 14 May 1831.
2. Quoted by Ciar Byrne in the *Guardian*, 19 May 2003.

bestowed upon her for protecting the oppressed.' Benjamin
Franklin

On 13 December 2005, Gordon Brown delivered the Hugo
Young memorial lecture on the subject of liberty and the
role of the State. Halfway through his speech, the Chancellor
referred to historian Gertrude Himmelfarb and her recent book,
The Roads to Modernity, in which she 'compares and contrasts the
contribution France, America and Britain made to the modern
world'.

'While France [. . .] had a revolution in the name of freedom,' quoted Brown, 'it is Britain and British ideas that led the
way into the modern world by focusing on benevolence, im-
provement of the civic society and the moral sense as necessary
for social progress.'

Though careful to choose the least controversial of Himmelfarb's statements, Labour's Gordon Brown was quoting from
one of the most ferociously neo-conservative pieces of revisionist
history to have been published recently. Himmelfarb has described the book as an 'ambitious attempt to reclaim the
Enlightenment [. . .] from the French who have dominated and
usurped it'. Enlightenment had nothing to do with France? I
guess Himmelfarb's next book will be on how the Italians
'usurped' the Renaissance.

Her basic analysis distinguishes between the good guys –
the British and the Americans – and the baddies, the French.
She argues that while the French in their demented pursuit
of abstraction were blinded by the tyranny of reason, the
enlightened Americans and British used religion and faith to
create a 'compassionate' conservatism, the only true form of
enlightenment.

Stephen E. Bronner from the *Washington Post* rightly put it:
'Himmelfarb wishes to show that President Bush's "coalition of

the willing" in Iraq has intellectual roots in the past. She depicts a libertarian Anglo-American philosophy with "social affections" that has bravely opposed the cynical and latently authoritarian hyper-rationalism of the French since the birth of modernity.' One reader on Amazon proposed the book be renamed *Reclaiming French Fries*.

Whatever was Gordon Brown thinking when he chose to quote from that book? Can you imagine Dominique de Villepin quoting from *The Little Red Book* and seeming to condone Mao's 'interesting' views on Britain and America?

In one sense, it is just the latest episode in the world's favourite soap opera, the one this trio has been acting out on the political stage since the mid-eighteenth century.

Let us forget Roosevelt, Churchill and de Gaulle. Forget Reagan, Thatcher and Mitterrand. Forget Bush, Blair and Chirac, or rather let's put them aside for a moment and go back to the beginning.

So when did it all start? I guess we must go back to the eighteenth century, a mere 250 years ago. Britain and France had been at each other's throats for centuries, when a delightfully energetic young newcomer in the British colonies dreamed of going solo. This young lad was a radical, he – or was it a she? – wanted to be able to speak his mind in the world without having to ask Old England's permission. Who could infant America turn to, to help break free from his chains? France and Spain surely? After all, both would do anything to counteract the influence of their common enemy, Britain. Both however, were monarchies and therefore more than a little concerned by young American ideas, a little too 'revolutionary' for their taste. Still, little by little, new winds began to blow across Europe. Thomas Jefferson and Tom Paine would count brave young French aristocrats with liberal ideas as equals. Enlightenment philosophers were already shaking the ground that Europe's absolute monarch had hoped to reign over for ever. For example:

In 1776, Tom Paine, an English-born intellectual and soon-to-be American citizen, published *Common Sense*, a powerful pamphlet dismissing monarchy, opposing slavery, calling for the end of British rule in America and the establishment of a republic. His ideas spread like wildfire and George Washington became one of his most ardent readers and admirers.

So, when Benjamin Franklin arrived in Versailles in 1778 to ask for France's money and army to help in America's War of Independence, he found a country ready and willing to oblige. The gangly seventy-year-old American hulk may have looked something of a peasant to his French hosts; nonetheless, he was introduced to Louis XVI as the 'Deputy of the United Provinces of North America'. A *débutante* America had just made its entrance on to the world stage.

The details of France's help to the American insurgents were thrashed out in heated conversations at balls and salons. Then, after signing treaties of friendship, trade and military alliances, France agreed to provide money and send ships and troops to North America. Historian Stacy Schiff in her book *Dr Franklin Goes to France* estimates that France gave away today's equivalent of $13 billion to its young American friend.[3] This generous gift almost bankrupted France. Some even say that the huge deficit it created paved the way for the French Revolution.

The War of Independence was a long and painful affair. Several times it looked as if Britain was going to overthrow the insurgents once and for all. The Marquis de Lafayette was among the young liberal French aristocrats who had made the American cause their own. Yet, despite Franco-American efforts, the British were still unyielding. Lafayette convinced Versailles to send more troops and more money. And then . . .

. . . General Washington, General de Rochambeau and Lord

3. *Dr Franklin Goes to France: How America Was Born in Monarchical Europe*, Stacy Schiff (Bloomsbury, 2005).

Cornwallis had an impromptu little meeting in Yorktown in the autumn of 1781. The world's favourite *ménage à trois* was born.

This is how American public broadcaster PBS reports the events of 19 October 1781 in its 'Liberty' series, a history of the American Revolution:

> In a stunning reversal of fortune that may signal the end of fighting in the American colonies, Charles Lord Cornwallis today signed orders surrendering his British army to a combined French and American force outside the Virginia tobacco port of Yorktown. Cornwallis's second-in-command, Charles O'Hara, attempted to deliver Cornwallis's sword to French general Comte de Rochambeau. But Rochambeau directed O'Hara to American general George Washington, who coolly steered the British officer to Washington's own second-in-command, Major General Benjamin Lincoln . . .

On its website, the French Embassy in Washington has a different way of telling the story, which is more flattering to the Americans:

> The defeated British army marched between the victors, the French to their right, the Americans to their left. British second-in-command, General O'Hara, represented Lord Cornwallis, who was taken ill. When O'Hara wanted to deliver Cornwallis's sword, he presented it first to Rochambeau. The French general directed O'Hara to Washington, who, respectful of the vanquished, refused it.

Whatever happened to Lord Cornwallis's sword, Britain had to bow its head. After lengthy negotiations a peace treaty was signed in Versailles on 3 September 1783, and the United States of America were born. France was the first country to recognise the new independent States. The liberal aristocrats who had fought for America's freedom now had urgent matters to attend to: France was on the boil. The Enlightenment was about to

give birth to yet another revolution, the bloodiest and perhaps
the most glorious: the French Revolution. All the while Thomas
Jefferson and Tom Paine – Americans in Paris throughout the
events – gorged themselves on new ideas and concepts and
praised the *révolutionnaires'* achievements. And, across the Channel, reactionaries such as Edmund Burke sharpened their quills.
But Britain had had its revolution in 1688 – so there was no need
to regress to an infantile state like the French and American
revolutionaries.

Ever since, the partners in the old *ménage à trois* have taken
turns to play the different roles at hand: the cheated husband, the
whimsical mistress and the irascible lover. Sometimes the three
have all been in love with each other at the same time.

Their continual squabbles are those of rivals or passionate
lovers. In both relationships, periods of intense admiration are
followed by ones of complete disenchantment. If the disenchantment sometimes feels irreversible, it's simply because their
expectations have been set so high from the beginning.

On the evening of 14 July 1989, on the roof of the Hôtel de
Crillon, where France was entertaining the world's leaders
during the bicentenary celebrations of the revolution, and just
moments before the formidable soprano Jessye Norman, draped
in a French flag designed by Tunisian Azzedine Alaia, was about
to appear lifted through the air singing 'La Marseillaise' at the
bottom of the Champs Elysées in front of 2 million people,
Margaret Thatcher pointed out to François Mitterrand, 'You
know, there is nothing so special about your revolution and
about beheading kings. We did it first, and that was a century
before you.' Ouch!

What really unnerved British reactionaries like Edmund
Burke was the time of the Terror, when the revolutionary ideals
were hijacked by a group of die-hard and bloodthirsty abstrac-
tionists. The French Revolution had now pushed the argument
so far that its ideas were treated as sacred. All religions and their

enslaving dogmas had been abolished only to be replaced by another one, atheist this time, called *la République*. And although the nineteenth and twentieth centuries gave France many different kinds of political regimes, the ideal of an atheist republic remained engraved in the national psyche until it was passed as a law in 1905. The Law of Separation between the State and the Church declares in its first article, 'The French Republic guarantees freedom of conscience.' The second article reads, 'The French Republic neither recognises nor supports any kind of religion.'

Never has there been such a thing in Britain or America. Religion has long been the most contentious subject between the three countries and often seems to be the base of their opposing visions of the world. In Britain, religion has always been seen as a guarantee of public order, a way of instilling virtue into the people that will prevent them from being too unruly. The monarch is the head of State and of the Church. British prime ministers such as Blair evoke Good and Evil in public without batting an eyelid. In the USA, the word 'sect' is no insult; on the contrary. Religion permeates every aspect of American life, hence American presidents' final 'God bless America' at the end of every speech. In France, such references are an anathema. In France, you are taught to believe that religion is bad, pernicious, in other words, bollocks – lies told by the powerful to enslave the gullible. Reason and scepticism are said to be the only road to spiritual elevation. Many French people receive a religious education at home or in their community, yet they usually keep it private and don't let it interfere with their politics.

Beyond religion, France and America, two republics born from the same ideas through two parallel revolutions, are so similar it's hard to spot the difference.

The Economist wrote:

The modern French and American politics may have evolved

quite differently, notably where the role of the State is concerned, but both emerged as highly codified, secular republics. Both – unlike the dissembling English – can articulate unapologetically what their country stands for [. . .] Within the same year, 1789, both the French Declaration of the Rights of Man and the American Bill of Rights were drafted. Above all, each nation believed in the universalism of its model – the Americans stressing liberty, the French civilisation – and shared an ambition to share it abroad.[4]

How true!

Long after Jefferson, Paine, Franklin and Lafayette had died, their legend grew and fed the imaginations of generations of Americans and French citizens. To mark *l'amitié franco-américaine*, France gave her young friend a gift, which when unveiled in 1886 became one of the most striking symbols of the brave new world, the Statue of Liberty, or rather *La Liberté éclairant le monde*, as it was originally titled.[5]

This Franco-American romance continued to blossom, for instrance, on 4 July 1917, American General Pershing, kneeling in front of Lafayette's grave in Paris, pronounced the three famous words *'Lafayette, nous voilà!'*. Then twenty-five years later, in Hollywood-produced *Casablanca*, Humphrey Bogart, the American cynic, and Claude Rains, the dubious Frenchman with a big heart, trick the Nazis together for the cause of freedom: 'I think this is the beginning of a beautiful friendship,' is Bogart's last line. But when, in January 1943, Roosevelt and de Gaulle met for the first time in Casablanca, their dislike was mutual. Luckily for all concerned, Winston Churchill accepted the role of go-between.

4. Christmas special issue, *The Economist*, 24 December 2005.
5. This translates as Liberty Enlightening the World. US President Cleveland unveiled it in 1886.

After the Second World War, as America became increasingly powerful, leftist French intellectuals nurtured an ambivalent anti-Americanism. They profoundly admired and loved American artists whilst violently reacting against what they saw as America's pernicious cultural imperialism. While Britain seemed accepting of all things American, the French started criticising *l'invasion américaine* in their daily lives, even if they did so while munching on American burgers. The French would soon find Britain's tendency to jump to attention whenever America clicked its fingers *vraiment pas virile*.

When, in 2003, France defied her once-adored America over Iraq, she realised she would mourn her lost love alone. Britain was not going to help her change America's mind. Britain had sided with America in the name of Good and Evil and against rationalist France. America, furious with her old lover to whom she owed her very existence, seemed to be wondering whether to ship that wedding anniversary gift, the Statue of Liberty, back to Paris.

What will the future bring for the world's favourite disconsolate lovers? Reconciliation does not seem impossible. After all, America and France recently spoke with one voice over the question of Lebanon and Syria. Soon, decisions about the future of Iraq will again be channelled through the United Nations, with France, the US and Britain seated at the same table again, side by side.

Britain may even start to see sense in France's insistence on building a strong Europe to counteract US supremacy and to offer an alternative vision for the world. The launch of Galileo could form the basis of Europe's technological independence. As in all modern relationships, independence is good; love must be given freely. But first, Britain's Chancellor must stop reading neo-conservative French-bashing nonsense.

3

Apologising

'This is Britain, where people apologise to lamp-posts after bumping into them.' Cassandra Jardine

The first time I heard somebody say to me, 'Oh, I'm *so awfully* sorry,' I thought they were taking the piss. When I realised they were deadly serious, I thought I'd better investigate. I'd write all 'expressions' I found strange in a little notebook I had entitled 'British Idiosyncrasies'.

'It's *terribly* kind of you' was followed by '*I'm afraid* I won't be able to come tonight,' '*I'm afraid* this is not quite right' and '*I'm afraid* dinner is a little overcooked.' I thought, Why are they constantly 'afraid'? Why do they have to use it at the beginning of every other sentence? I knew it actually meant, 'I regret that' . . . and yet still it sounded strange to my foreign ear. I thought, I'm not afraid of being late; I *will* be late. Does it feel any better to be afraid?

Then I discovered the double negatives, a whole new chapter in my notebook. 'I would never want not to see you.' Does he mean he loves me? 'I don't disagree with you.' Does he *actually agree* with me? 'He is not incompetent.' Why can't she say that he *is* competent? I thought, Gosh, what a convoluted way of expressing oneself. In France, we're not afraid, we don't use double negatives, or at least very rarely, and we're never 'awfully sorry'. You'll be lucky if we are even simply sorry for the wrong we might have done you.

I soon learned that this way of talking was a game and, an act of class. I sometimes found it hard to meet a British person with an average degree of politeness, as language seemed to be polarised between these two extremes: excessively polite and downright crass. Wasn't there a middle ground between 'Awfully sorry, dear' and 'Fuck you, you fucking retard'?

In France, no such extremes, just refined mass rudeness. Democratic and classless impudence, another legacy of the revolution.

I must admit that, at first, it felt extremely nice to be asked something so nicely. What civilised people, I thought. Ah, English courtesy . . . Whenever friends came to dinner, they'd write a thank-you card. What elegance, what *savoir-vivre*! Everybody always asked me what I wanted to do, what I wanted to eat, drink, what film I wanted to see, etc. My mistake, of course, was to tell them what I really wanted.

In this social game of words, the first rule is never to tell the truth, or at least never directly. Nobody was ever really 'awfully sorry' in most cases where I observed its use, and, other times, when they truly were, they didn't need to say so, as sincerity always has a way of showing. I didn't play the game very well. I found it tedious. Politeness is good, to a certain extent, but too much of it verges on hypocrisy.

Whatever they have to say, the English bourgeoisie cloak their words in politeness, especially if the intention is to insult. They always start with the traditional preliminary warning, 'I'm sorry,' then off goes the insult: 'I'm sorry to say you're a real bastard' or, even better, 'I'm sorry I ever met you.' Even if, in fact, 'I'm sorry' is not actually an apology as such for the speaker, it still sounds so to continental ears. It is as if the most important thing is to deliver the insult within required propriety, i.e. *dans les formes*.

I simply love witnessing the joust of double negatives and innuendos, especially in exchanges laden with class antagonism. I remember this scene from a gem of a film *Agatha*, directed by Michael Apted in 1979, with Vanessa Redgrave and Dustin Hoffman in the leading roles. Working-class Deputy Chief Constable Kenwood, played by Timothy West, meets upper-class Colonel Christie, played by Timothy Dalton. Kenwood has his men searching the lake where Agatha Christie might have drowned. Her deceitful and hateful husband doesn't want any bad publicity and couldn't care less about his wife's whereabouts. From the moment they shake hands, the contempt between the two men is both obvious and mutual.

CHRISTIE: What's going on?

KENWOOD: We're dragging the pool, sir.

CHRISTIE: What for?

KENWOOD: Purely routine, sir.

CHRISTIE: I hope it's not a case of excessive zeal on your part, Kenwood.

KENWOOD: I assure you, just routine, no cause for alarm.

CHRISTIE: I would strongly urge you in your own interest to call all this off.

KENWOOD: Why would you say that, sir?

CHRISTIE: I wouldn't want you to make a fool of yourself, Kenwood.

KENWOOD: It's very considerate of you, Colonel. Thank you, sir.

Seen from France, this is what we would call a civilised slanging match *à l'anglaise*. A similar exchange in French would be shorter and more direct. Confrontation and unleashed emotions are usually the prevailing mode of communication in France, while, in the UK, inner tension dominates social intercourse.

It's difficult to find the origin of the English bourgeoisie's double-edged politeness. Perhaps it stems partly from the national addiction to self-deprecation. It seems that if you are born into the English middle class, you must apologise for everything you do, everything you say, even for everything you are. Of course it is a game, one of the most arrogant actually and not one that should be taken seriously, but some people, foreigners in particular, often take it at face value. Hence the English reputation for great politeness but also for a seeming reluctance to stand up for any principles they may have, except in extreme circumstances when they rise magnificently. When the British apologise constantly for what they stand for (culture, traditions, values, etc.), even if it is only a game, they ought to remember that they might be taken seriously. It is sometimes better to appear more principled and ruder; it is less misleading, especially in times of international turmoil.

There seems to be a crucial difference between saying sorry and apologising. The national game since 2003 has been, or so it has seemed to the foreign observer, to guess when Tony Blair would apologise to the country for having involved Britain in a war its people didn't want. We are still waiting, it seems. Maybe he should learn how to say sorry without apologising. In France, politicians have got the knack: they admit they are 'responsible' but claim they are 'not guilty' . . . Another wordplay.

Speaking one's mind seems such a rare thing in Britain that when I read an interview with singer Mick Hucknall, I thought it was kind of refreshing, even if the style somehow lacked finesse:

'I am one of the best songwriters this country has produced. Ever. If people don't like me saying that, tough shit. People should deal with facts. People who feign modesty are wankers. They're the biggest fakes. It almost makes my blood boil. I'm a Northerner; I like things to be real. They are not like that in the South.'[1]

---

1. Quoted in the *Observer*, 5 February 2006.

However, I'm still waiting to meet English people who are moderately polite: sorry when they are sorry, but not 'gonna-fucking-kill-ya' if I inadvertently jump the queue.

4

Culture

'Cultural exception is not negotiable.' Catherine Trautmann[1]

Remember, it seems like only yesterday. The early 1990s, GATT talks, the Uruguay Round.[2] Teeth clenched, muscles taut as a bowstring, negotiators tried to contain themselves in front of the press, but things looked grim. Away from the cameras, in the corridors, the very same people were shouting abuse at each other. A battle was being played out on the backstage of global business.

World trade negotiations had been in progress for some time, the talks were taking place at a painfully slow pace, when suddenly everybody had frozen, speechless. *Le deadlock*, the impasse. The discussion had come to the topic of the arts and culture, i.e. cultural goods and services. The Americans had thought it went without saying that they would be included in all negotiations about liberalisation of world trade and investment. European leaders had tried to bide their time and had ventured to say that, well, they'd rather leave it aside for the time being. The

1. French Minister for Culture speaking during the GATT negotiations in 1999.
2. General Agreement on Tariffs and Trade which became the WTO (World Trade Organization) in 1994.

USA reformulated their question and this time *demanded* the arts be included. Their tone now suddenly showed that there was, at least in their mind, no other option but for the Europeans to oblige. Europe replied, fearful of what might come and wavering slightly, 'Well, yes, we hear you, but couldn't we possibly talk about it later?' The Americans looked uncomprehending and started rolling up their sleeves. Then the French stepped forward and announced bluntly, 'Non.'

Oh.

Why am I choosing this particular episode of international trade to illustrate the profound difference between the French, British and American perspective on the arts? Simply because it illustrates differences in the meaning of arts for the three cultures perfectly.

Negotiators at the Uruguay Round, like the businessmen they are, were discussing matters of global trade – you know, oil, cereals, gas, cocoa, car manufacturing, etc. – when the c-word was uttered. And suddenly all hell broke loose. Businessmen and their lawyers became boxers in a ring. We had touched a nerve and it was a big one, the most sensitive of all. At least for the French, who put on their armour and sharpened their tongues. The French fundamentally believed that culture and cultural exports could not be treated and traded in the same way as you would any other commodity because national cultures were to be protected and preserved. Culture was the exception to the rule! Culture could not be traded like toothpaste, or, if it ever was, it would be over their dead bodies. And they meant it.

The arts and culture play an essential part in the French psyche. In France, an artist stands above all; his or her art is seen as a gift to the nation, hence the unique system of unemployment benefit to all artists and technicians working in the arts. If they can prove that they have worked 570 hours in the year, they are entitled to a regular (and handsome) state allowance. The idea is to enable them to pursue and perfect their art on a full stomach. Want another example of the unique status of the artist in France? When the writer Jean Genet appeared in court in 1943 for theft, he faced life imprisonment for recidivism. Jean Cocteau wrote a letter to the court, which was read publicly: 'He is Rimbaud; one cannot convict Rimbaud.' The question was never whether Genet was guilty or not, but whether the law could possibly convict a genius. The answer was *non, évidemment.* Genet walked away a free man.

In France, when an artist talks, the nation listens. If an artist also turns out to be an intellectual, well, the gates of heaven open wide for him. The expression 'to live like God in France' should really be 'to live like an artist in France'. Have you seen the film *The Taste of Others*, directed by Agnès Jaoui? It tells the story of a businessman who longs to be an artist. He doesn't mind becoming poor; what he is dreaming of is the consideration an artist gets. But only in France. In the UK, artists are not gods, but they are cool, especially if they go on television, appear in *Hello!*, look cool, act cool and earn a lot of money. If they talk about politics, they are boring and ridiculous, like Harold Pinter. In France, Pinter is a god.

Arts and culture are two sides of the same French coin. French education is obsessed with *culture générale* which loosely translates as general knowledge. Professional and vocational schools are for mediocre pupils or gifted specialists. However, *la crème de la crème* go on to *grandes écoles* to perfect their *culture générale*. This *crème* will become know-it-all generalists, able to talk about anything and everything for about . . . ten minutes. Becoming a specialist is what you end up doing only if you were unlucky. In the UK, what's good is what works, and since it is almost impossible to know how everything works, you specialise in a subject at school, take your exams and then (hopefully) get a job in that field. A specialist knows his stuff, though he might miss the broader picture. In France, we know all about the broader picture but nothing of the finer details!

In the UK, the word 'culture' doesn't mean much (and if it does, it usually means 'anthropology'). Just look at the British Department for Culture: nobody talks about it or takes it seriously. It is the cram-it-all-in ministry, in charge of the arts, sports, the National Lottery, heritage, media and . . . tourism. So the whole debate about 'cultural exception' back in 1993 must have seemed slightly odd to the British negotiators.

I was a student in Paris then. I could hear the world trade negotiators' doors slamming shut in my bedroom. I could see the arm-wrestling taking place on my dining-room table. It must have been one of the last times that France said *non* to the USA. I mean the last time before the invasion of Iraq. What France was saying, supported by the majority of her European partners, with a very doubtful Britain, was simple: culture and arts are not goods like any other. A film is not like a can of Coke and cannot be treated as such. Culture and the arts must be placed outside the realm of laissez-faire. Britain discreetly disengaged from the issue, both being and feeling half in and half out of Europe. She watched Paris and Washington at each other's throats with some delight.

Cinema and the film industry were at the heart of the dispute. Though the French may have invented cinema, the Americans mass-produced it. Is cinema art, or is it a business like any other? Does cinema present ideas? Does it enlighten people as well as entertain them? And can it *foment* revolutions? The French argued that cinema was an art form whose masterpieces were as worthy of being exhibited in the Louvre as Michelangelo's paintings. 'Baloney,' replied the Americans. 'Cinema is money. It gives pleasure as much as a Mars bar; the people who make cinema are manufacturers, like Ford car manufacturers, not artists.' France replied, 'Can't you see that your Orson Welles, Billy Wilder, John Ford and our Vigo, Renoir and Truffaut are great artists? Each of their films is a unique prototype like the *Venus de Milo*, and not a Model T Ford anybody can reproduce.'

The USA should have known that the European partners had spent three long years, between 1986 and 1989, agreeing on exactly that. From their debate emerged the common audiovisual policy called Television Without Frontiers. Recognising the uniqueness of films, and all cultural goods, the policy aimed to develop and sustain the production, financing and distribution of national and European films within the EU. Every nation could impose, should they wish, quotas on national broadcasters in order to promote European culture. For instance, French broadcasters must by law show at least 60% European films (out of which 40% must be in French). Quotas being recommendations and not compulsory, each country could apply them as they saw fit. These long years of discussions had brought the different European partners, with their different traditions, closer together. A common spirit was taking shape, fragile but nevertheless real.

When GATT talks started in February 1993, the USA simply assumed that the liberalisation of cultural goods and services was a sure thing and that European countries would dismantle all the old-fashioned cultural institutions that were financing their local film industries. Everything would be for the best, and, surely, all Europeans would welcome market-winning Hollywood films with open arms. Why should Europe want to resist the obvious? Resistance was a thing of the past, reserved for backward people, the sun-tanned Californians seemed to imply.

Well, Europe, led by the vocal French, did resist, shakily at first, but she then gained momentum and found support for her combat. More and more countries out of the 117 GATT members agreed with her stance. Jack Valenti, the powerful president of the Motion Picture Association of America, beside himself with rage, described the Europeans' position as a 'real cancer'. What is striking is that the USA hadn't expected such a turn of events. They were talking market; Europe was talking philosophy.

Ah.

Had Europe obeyed the master of the market, one well produced, well financed and well distributed vision would have covered the planet like a warm, suffocating blanket.

To neo-fascists who keep telling us that Europe has never had an identity but is merely an amalgam of former enemies, the GATT debate and outcome must have come as a surprise. Even more so because the majority of the world actually agreed with that vision.

And to those who shouted that France was playing her cards selfishly, let us remind them that the 'cultural exception' was not in any way a 'French exception'. Some commentators played on words and claimed that France was simply defending her '*culture exceptionnelle*'. According to them, France was trying to impose her Stalinist protectionism on the world. Bollocks. Nor was exception ever meant as an exclusion. In fact, the expression 'cultural exception' meant defending the right of every nation to 'cultural diversity'.

The talks lasted fourteen months, and, on 15 April 1994, a global trade agreement was signed, leaving aside cultural goods and services, thus recognising their separate nature. Britain had very discreetly moved towards France and her European partners.

However, there was no time for celebration and very little respite. A year later, in May 1995, the twenty-nine members of the Organisation for Economic Cooperation and Development (OECD) met in Château de la Muette near Paris to discuss the Multilateral Agreement on Investment (MAI). The aim: to reach an agreement on the liberalisation of direct investment, a protection for transnational investors – i.e. any investor wishing to invest in a foreign country would not be subject to national quotas or any kind of performance requirements.

Broadly applied to the audiovisual and cultural sector, such an agreement meant that a Hollywood studio with, say, a subsidiary in a European country would have been eligible for national and European subsidies while escaping broadcasting quotas. In the publishing world, it would have meant that a foreign investor wouldn't have had to respect European intellectual property laws, etc. Taken to its logical conclusion, the MAI would eventually dissolve all national social, cultural, environmental and health policies.

Needless to say, discussions soon became heated, especially on the cultural front. France, backed by Canada, Belgium, Italy, Greece and Portugal, asked that the hard-fought-for principle of 'cultural exception' be maintained. Endless talks and consultations took place. In fact, the Americans also wanted to make a few exceptions to the rule they had invented. They wanted to reserve the right to deny national subsidies to foreign investors, the very principle they had originally demanded. They also reserved the right to 'punish' foreign investors wishing to invest in 'outlaw' countries such as Cuba and Iran. In February 1998, talks were adjourned. When, in October 1998, talks resumed, Prime Minister Lionel Jospin decided France wouldn't take part. The guillotine had fallen. That was the end of the MAI.

The ultra-liberals and free-marketeers had lost a battle but not the entire war, which they intended to win at all costs. They decided they would contain the European plague of cultural exception and its policy of quotas by intimidating new countries wishing to join international organisations such as the OECD and the World Trade Organisation (WTO): they told these states they would receive the support of Washington when they applied but only if they made sure they 'forgot' to sign the cultural exception paragraph when they did. Open up your film market to us and you'll be Washington's friends. Countries from the ex-Soviet bloc made ideal targets. The only problem, of course, was that if these states then wanted to apply for EU membership, they would face strong opposition from the EU, as potential members must embrace all EU regulations, the cultural exception being one of them. Romania proved to be the first headache. She became a member of the WTO with Washington's help. But when she applied to become an EU member, it was discovered she had forgotten to sign the cultural exception paragraph . . . Europe struck back: Romania had to choose where her heart really lay. Washington protested.

Throughout these events, Britain had been watching, from the sidelines, deciding what to do. For once, she wasn't persuaded that Washington knew better. Recently, Britain chose sides, like 148 other countries. On 21 October 2005, eleven years after the Uruguay Round, the general conference of the United Nations Educational, Scientific and Cultural Organisation (UNESCO) met in Paris and approved the Convention on the Protection and Promotion of the Diversity of Cultural Expression, an international normative instrument that came into force three months later. Two countries opposed it: the USA and Israel. This convention recognises states' rights 'to maintain, adopt and implement policies and measures they deem appropriate for the protection and promotion of the diversity of cultural expressions on their territory'.

On the night of its birth, the BBC asked me to comment on the historical vote on Radio 4's *World Tonight*. With me was Louise Oliver, US ambassador to UNESCO. When asked by British broadcaster Robin Lustig whether the convention meant Europeans wouldn't be able to see American films if they wished, I replied, 'It won't prevent them from seeing American films if they desire; it will simply allow them to see all other films that are not American.' Lustig went on teasing me, 'What about foie gras? There are talks about making it a cultural exception too.' 'And why not?' I replied. The US ambassador had little time for jokes. She claimed that the law was 'flawed' and 'in breach of the Universal Declaration of Human Rights'. Robin Lustig replied,

'You mean, Ambassador, the human right to see a Hollywood film?'

Cultural exception and British irony stole the show . . . until the next onslaught.

5

Buy, Buy, Buy

'Perhaps the bargain-hunting pilgrims are not the vanguard of a new age of consumerist fundamentalism but a manifestation of the post-religious world's immaturity.' Julian Baggini, commentator

'I wouldn't say I was an obsessive shopper, but the chance to come to Italy and go shopping without the family is my idea of heaven. I can do culture with my husband.' Caroline Forman, a recruitment manager with an eighteen-month-old daughter[1]

This can't be a coincidence: I'm writing these lines on the first day of the sales in Britain. Funny that the winter sales should start the day after Christmas: two whole days of rituals and religious fervour, one celebrating the love of Jesus, the other the mother of all Bargains. Judging by the relative length of queues outside shops and churches in the UK, I have the feeling that there may be more followers of the latter than the former. This comes as no surprise: Britain being the most 'de-Christianised' country in Europe, it seems only natural that the official religion should have been superseded by worship of another Holy Trinity: shop, shop, shop.

1. Quoted by Barbara McMahon, the *Observer*, 13 November 2005.

Shopping is a British institution; it is a word almost universally recognised everywhere on the planet. Just as some people would give their lives for their religious or political beliefs, others are ready to die for a 50%-off tag. There are hordes of the latter species in the UK. Think I'm going too far? Just remember the midnight opening of the new Ikea in Edmonton, North London in February 2005: five people were injured and around twenty suffered from heat exhaustion. This is how the *Guardian* reported it at the time: 'It's happened again. People have been "trampled by surging queues", leaving officials "deeply shocked, upset and concerned". One woman "pushed her way forward, screaming with excitement". There was a "crush" and a "scramble". "It was a stampede," according to one eyewitness. "You couldn't reason with these people: they were out of control." '[2] According to police reports, bargain-hunters even abandoned their cars on the busy A406 North Circular, causing severe traffic problems. The London Ambulance Service declared that advertising for cut-price offers over 24 hours had attracted between 4,000 and 6,000 people to the Ikea store.

'In Middlesbrough, John Allan, 60, began queuing outside furniture retailer Barker and Stonehouse at 1.30 p.m. on Christmas Day to buy a sofa reduced from £2,520 to £399 at 10 a.m. on Boxing Day.'[3] They don't say whether the poor man stood outside for twenty hours and thirty minutes or whether he had brought his tent to camp on the pavement.

'In Aberdeen, shopper Jane MacDonald, 34, left her house at midnight to be first in line at Next, and stood in the rain for five hours before the shop opened. After that, she still had to queue at

---

2. Julian Baggini, the *Guardian*, 11 February 2005. He admitted using quotes from the actual event but also from other stampedes, which took place during pilgrimages in India and Saudi Arabia, in order to make the same point as me.

3. Hugh Muir, the *Guardian*, 27 December 2005.

the tills for almost two hours with hundreds of other shoppers.'[4]
No doubt she had an umbrella, a folding chair, warm clothes, a
thermos of tea and a few biscuits to keep her going. I'm sure she
did: the British are always well prepared for outdoor activities.

Despite what you may think, I'm not trying to depict the
British as a nation of raving shopaholics – far from it. There are
as many fashion victims in France, or Italy, and bargain-hunting
is widely practised across the Channel. However, there is something terribly British about the sheer act of consuming. In the
UK, to spend is good; I mean morally good for you – it's called
retail therapy – and morally good for the country, as your
Chancellor keeps telling you. Your cousin George W. Bush
recently said it was 'patriotic'. Well, it's certainly Keynesian, and
Keynes was British.

In the UK, one can now shop almost all the time. In the late
1990s, I saw the first of Sainsbury's 24/7 giant supermarkets
open in Central London, like the one in Camden Town where I
lived for two years. I was fascinated; I thought, Great! This is
like America! In France, shops are closed on Sunday, usually
Monday too, two hours over lunchtime, plus a hefty five weeks
during the summer. Only food shops were – and still are – open
on Sunday mornings, and cafés, of course. As a child, I loathed
Sundays, too depressing and uneventful for my taste, apart from
the visit to the pâtisserie. How I enjoy French Sundays now. A
time when I'm free from the temptation to consume. At least
there is one day in the week when money is not an issue, when I
can pretend not to know how poor I am.

That's the thing; in the UK, even poor people can buy. Hence
the dreaded credit trap. I discovered credit cards in England.
You see, in France what we call *cartes de crédit* are actually debit
cards. There is no right to an overdraft, unless you've negotiated
it with your bank. I was brought up never to borrow money

4. *Ibid.*

from the bank. I was only to buy things I could afford. However, I was also brought up to be curious to taste and try all things new. So I decided that I was going to 'taste' *la vie à crédit*. Giving in to the many bank offers, which plopped on to the doormat every other day, I applied for a credit card and learned to live the English way, running up heaps of debt every month on which I paid colossal interest.

To spend gives you status; if you spend, it means you've got money, the ultimate measure of success in today's Britain. The curves and trends of retail profits are scrutinised every month in the same feverish way as the housing market. If retail figures drop by 0.3%, the whole country is overcome with dread. If they pick up again the following month, phew, life's OK. When the winter sales loom, everybody holds their breath: will records be broken again? Will figures plunge? Will the Bank of England intervene and lower interest rates to boost retail profit? Every newspaper in the country provides pre-sales guides on how to catch the best buys in the high-street stores or on retailers' websites, on opening hours and exchange and refund policies.

No such thing in France. There are sales, of course, but no frenzied activity. There are no guides on how to hunt down better bargains than your neighbour, no special minibus hire to transport your purchases, no free massages for marathon shoppers who have reached the £1,000 mark in less than an hour. As for the policy of returning unwanted items, this has only become possible in the last ten years. I grew up in a country where, once sold, a sale item was *non-échangeable*, *non-remboursable* even if you discovered that the garment you had just bought was damaged. *Le shopping à la française* was at your own peril. Even brand-new items could only be exchanged and never refunded. I learned to shop the hard way. Here lies the main difference between our two countries: treatment of the customer.

In the UK, as indeed in the United States, the customer is at best a king, at worst a client. The first trip any French citizen makes to an American shopping mall leaves them in culture shock. French visitors are in awe: servile sales assistants, all flashing white teeth, greeting you warmly and asking how you are 'today'. Such service is unheard of in France.

In France, you're rarely welcome in a shop or a café, or, for that matter, anywhere you need to be served. Recently, I was having a coffee with a friend in Le Bûcheron café in the St-Paul area of Paris. A guy behind the bar was making crêpes. We asked for a crêpe with our *café crème*. '*Non*', replied our young waiter. I asked why. He replied that crêpes were only served to people who ordered the full brunch menu. I tried, as I always do – I'm French after all – to be Cartesian: 'Look, your colleague is making crêpes, they look great. We'll eat them quickly, charge us whatever you want and we won't tell the boss. It's money straight in the till.' '*Non*,' came the answer, 'but you can have chocolate tart.' '*Non*,' I replied, exerting my own French right to utter the n-word. 'What I want is a crêpe.' He shrugged his shoulders and departed, leaving us to ponder our next move. I was ready to make a fuss in public, but my English friend laughed and shrugged his shoulders too. French intransigence vs. British indifference. I gave in and had the chocolate tart.

Three days ago, I was in another Parisian café. I asked for a club sandwich with green beans instead of chips. The waiter said, '*Non, impossible*. The cook will refuse to serve anything other than chips with a club sandwich.' I argued that I had been served green beans with my club sandwich a few weeks earlier at the very same table. '*Non, impossible*,' he repeated. Being accompanied by a French friend this time, I made a fuss and insisted on seeing the cook. He said that last time he had made an exception to the rule. Well, could he make an exception again? He reflected for a moment, stared at the ceiling, deep in thought, and said finally, 'As an exception, yes.'

In both cases, we were dealing with matters of principle. For both waiter and cook, it didn't matter if their attitudes meant they'd lose money, or even customers; there couldn't be a higher cause than the principles upon which their menu had been drawn up. However, an exception was possible in the second case because it didn't shake the foundations. Indeed, *l'exception confirme la règle*. France is a country founded on principles with many exceptions to the rule.

To get what you want in a French shop may feel like you are playing chess with a formidable opponent. The sales people have tricks up their sleeves you would never have dreamt of. Recently, I was walking down boulevard Beaumarchais, the long main road between Bastille and République, a shopping area that specialises in photographic equipment. I was looking for a red filter to give as a Christmas present. I opened the door of the nearest shop. Its windows – full of bits and pieces, new and second-hand Rolleiflex, Leicas, automatic novelties and so on – looked interesting. Good enough for me. I asked for a 39 mm red filter, and, after much fiddling in boxes and glass cabinets, I was presented with . . . a yellow filter. It was the right size and seemed fine, except I wanted a red one. I asked whether they had any. The shopkeeper, genuinely nice, said, 'Oh, yes, we do have red filters, but yellow is better: it's *universel*.' Well, if it's *universel* . . . what can one say? Nothing, nothing at all. I bought it and said '*merci*' to the shop owner who had sold me something I didn't want. I then had to explain to the person who had asked for a red filter for Christmas that, honestly, yellow was much better. In France, words are important. The word *Universel* is a Taser gun: it leaves you paralysed, speechless, unable to retaliate. Hoist the white flag!

In France, the customer is never king – and if ever they are treated like royalty, this must be an exception to the rule. Customers are seen by traders as irritating people best ignored and got rid of as quickly as possible. As an English friend who had recently settled in the French capital pointed out to me, 'I now know what the "N" on public buildings stands for! It's not

for "Napoleon", it's for *"Non"*, *"N'y en a plus"*,[5] *"Ne sert plus"*.[6]
Touché!

So why treat a client badly? Surely such behaviour undermines profits and may even end in bankruptcy? One has to look at the nature of capitalism in France to get the beginning of an answer. In France, as in Italy, capitalism is still often based on the family, a system sustained by intricate legislation. There are still many independent and family-owned trades. In essence, a customer is a bore because they invade the owner's living space. If the owner of a shop is having a bad hair day, he or she reserves the right to be rude or may simply refuse to sell. Money not being the ultimate measure of success in France, when shop or restaurant owners have earned what they deem enough to pay the bills, they may choose to turn away customers, close earlier than the official trading hours or leave on a five-week holiday. If you're not happy and let them know, they will shrug. What do they care? *La vie est ailleurs* – life is elsewhere.

However, in the past ten years, France has experienced franchise development at the speed of lightning. Customers are treated better in franchised shops, even in a monotonous and anonymous tone, simply because the people working in franchises are employees of big corporations with headquarters in Chicago, Los Angeles or Milton Keynes, they treat customers badly, they get the sack. You feel wanted as a client, you're listened to, you feel somehow empowered. They even care for your custom. In other words, they need you. The flipside is that the uniformity quickly becomes nauseating. What you buy is a brand worn by millions of people; it's affordable and may be well cut. Sure, this is progress but, oh how you long for something 'different'. But this something 'different', 'original', 'unique' is now only within the reach of the super rich.

5. Translates as 'none left'.
6. 'Not serving.'

After having lived in the UK for ten years, I have got used to relatively good service wherever I shop. Yet, no matter how irritated pig-headed shopkeepers in France make me, I can't help but like their 'independent' spirit. They are their own boss. What's more, they treat everybody the same, be you a beggar or a lord. That's the one good thing about rudeness *universelle*.

6

Café Society

'It is a fair bet that the likes of Hemingway, Fitzgerald, Sartre and de Beauvoir would not have become the giants of world literature they are today had they been fuelled by Starbucks' takeaway caffè lattes rather than shots of strong espresso in such celebrated Left Bank cafés as Flore and Les Deux Magots.'
Jon Henley[1]

'Do you remember the first time you ever set foot in a café?' asked my six-year-old nephew. 'I think I will always remember the moment I order my first espresso,' he continued solemnly. Strange as it sounds, no, I don't remember *la première fois*, but my nephew is right; I should remember, as it must be, in the French psyche, almost as important as the first time one falls in love.

I do remember, however, from a very early age, going to a café with my dad, who would stand, not sit, at the counter, knocking back his *p'tit noir* in record time, sometimes grabbing a boiled egg from the metal pyramidal rack and cracking the shell on the *zinc*.[2] At the time, sitting in a café seemed reserved for

1. The *Guardian*, 26 September 2003.
2. Parisian cafés' counters are usually made of zinc, hence the metonymy 'to have a coffee at the zinc'.

44

people with time on their hands or lovers stealing moments together. Everything ordered and eaten at the counter was, and still is, much cheaper than anything served at a table.

Sitting in a café was a rarity. I remember vividly how, as a little girl, after occasional blood tests I had to endure early in the morning on an empty stomach, my *maman* would take me to a nearby café for a hot chocolate and a croissant to reward my bravery: total luxury. I felt like the Queen of Sheba.

I also remember how my eldest brother, a strikingly handsome intellectual and one of the three heroes in my life (along with my other brother and Gene Kelly), would leave home in the morning without breakfast. I was seven, he was twenty, and *Monsieur* would have his breakfast in a café: 'Make it a large black coffee with a pot of hot water on the side and a *tartine*, please.'[3] He would read the newspaper, scribble down cryptic thoughts on his notepad and the café's paper napkins, and then leave to go about his day. My mother thought it was a waste of money, but I was fascinated; this had to be what life was all about. One day, I'd do just the same. For me, there was nothing more desirable and symbolic than having coffee and a *tartine* in a café every morning; an incredible privilege, a sign of independence, wealth and personal fulfilment, thus surely the climax of one's existence.

I remember going to cafés with my *lycée* friends at the age of fifteen. We would sit (such extravagance) but order only coffee, the cheapest beverage available. We stayed for hours, gossiping, debating and sometimes canoodling in the red leather booths. When I became a student on the Left Bank, I'd sometimes spend my daily lunch allowance of 35ff on either a matinée cinema ticket or a *grand café crème* and *Le Monde* in the expensive and historical St-Germain-des-Prés cafés. It was silly, vain maybe, for a time, absolutely irresistible. I loved the Balzar on

3. A *tartine* is a buttered half baguette, cut in half.

rue des Ecoles, a small brasserie that hasn't changed since the 1930s and to which Sorbonne professors still go between lectures.

I used to go to Le Vieux Colombier, on the corner of rue de Rennes and rue du Vieux Colombier, where again *le décor*, with undulating curves on its ceiling and jewel-like lighting, hasn't changed since the art deco years. I'd go regularly in the afternoon to revise between two *confs*,[4] and, one day, at the next table, I spotted Lauren Bacall. I froze, can't remember how long my *rêverie* lasted, but when I finally snapped out of it, my *café crème* was stone cold. It was 1994, she wore trousers like nobody had ever worn them before: so chic I could have died. I bumped into her a few more times in the same café and each time I was mesmerised, enchanted: Hollywood was kissing me on the lips.

I also ventured to Les Deux Magots, opposite St-Germain-des-Prés Church. I had to. I couldn't not go. I wanted to sit where Sartre and de Beauvoir had sat, and where the legendary New Wave actor Jean-Pierre Léaud had perched nervously in *La Maman et la Putain*, Jean Eustache's 1972 masterpiece. The first time I went was also the last. I remember sitting down, looking around and waiting eagerly. Waiting for something to happen: a bolt of lightning, love at first sight, I don't know, anything. Nothing happened. The place was filled with Texan tourists, not a single French soul. I felt really stupid. I never set foot in there again. A few years ago, I got a call from a film producer who wanted us to meet. She suggested we go to Les Deux Magots. A shiver ran down my spine. I made up an excuse: I was busy this week after all, I was sorry, I would call again. But I never did. The world of cafés is fraught with danger; choose carefully, don't get it wrong or you might lose your good reputation. It's fragile, you know.

When I packed my bags to go and live in Britain, as a Parisian, I had priorities. First of all, I'd try all the cafés in a

4. Short for 'lecture'.

kilometre of my work and home and choose the one that would become *mine*, the one whose owner would soon know my name and serve me what I wanted without having to ask, the one where I'd meet friends, colleagues and where I'd write, work, make calls, read, think. Back in 1995, I had no idea of what a typical English street looked and felt like. If worst came to worst and I couldn't find a decent café, I didn't mind swapping my café for a teashop or a pub; I just needed a place to go to every day, like an extension of my bedroom.

Though I was adamant about wanting to do things locally, I soon had to forget about pubs as potential café substitutes: they don't open early enough, stink of beer, don't serve good coffee, and if you ask whether they serve brioche, they either burst out laughing or tell you to eff off. You may even end up with a dart in the book you're reading. As for teashops, too few and far between, too quaint, too unreal. Back to square one: coffee shop.

Luckily for me, in 1995, café culture had just taken off. In a few years, cafés sprang up from concrete pavements like mushrooms in the New Forest. Britain embraced café culture with the passion of the newly converted, accepting all and often failing to discern the good from the bad. Newspapers ran headlines such as 'Le café est arrivé!'[5] A new dawn had broken for Britain, and the early morning dew tasted good, or so it seemed.

Consciously or not, the British had chosen to import a part of the continental way of life; no doubt in order to enjoy the sparse rays of sunshine, to lounge like lizards on the newly created café terraces, meet friends before going out, sit and talk instead of standing, drinking and shouting in a pub.

This cultural revolution, taking place every day on the streets of London and Britain, felt weird to me, perhaps because it was so alien to British custom. My first experiences of 'British cafés' were in Café Rouge, Café Pélican and the Dôme. Of course, I

5. The *Guardian*, 23 April 1999.

had no preconceived ideas; I tried them all. I didn't know they were chains until I started seeing their identical twins all over London: same furniture, same menu, same food, same international student staff. Here one day, gone the next. However hard I tried, it just didn't work for me. I wasn't looking for a convenient place to have the same caffè latte every day; I was looking for a second home, run by people who cared, with simple carefully selected products and above all, without unnecessary frills. I then tried Pâtisserie Valérie in Central London; ouch – for my taste, unsubtle and extremely greasy croissants. One bite and I could feel my cholesterol rocketing.

Then came the waves of American coffee with the Seattle Coffee Company and Coffee Republic. Then *soi-disant* Italian companies Costa Coffee, Caffè Aroma and Caffè Nero with their caffè machiatto, fat-free blueberry muffins and loyalty cards. Again, I tried them all. I knew they were chains, but I naïvely hoped I might find a friendly branch with nice staff I could stick to. How wrong I was. The employees of these franchises seemed to work only for one crazy week and off they went, replaced by another gang of energetic international students learning economics the hard way. No time to get to know them; they'd all vanish before we, the clients, could even read the names on their badges. There we stayed, left behind, forlorn. 'My waiter left me for another franchise' – why haven't the tabloids run that headline yet?

However, that was the Belle Epoque; the good old days. All that took place in a dreamy idyllic world. A world before the great onslaught struck; the one that will no doubt submerge us all. September 1998, one of the darkest moments in the history of Britain: Starbucks invaded Britain's shores. You think I'm overdoing it? One day, you will remember my words.

I was familiar with the thirty-year-old company from my trips to America and had no misgivings about it. America had always been notoriously bad for its coffee, known in France as *jus de chaussettes*, sock juice. That a company should want to provide better-quality coffee to Americans seemed like a good idea. Starbucks looked quintessentially American, with its fat-free cookies, dairy-free latte, soya-milk decaf espresso, easy music and plastic décor with a few leather armchairs. They were successful? Good for them. The next thing I heard made unsettling reading, though: they were opening outlets all over the world. A Starbucks opened on Tiananmen Square in Beijing. The first in China, it sounded funny at first, though with hindsight I now realise it wasn't.

We didn't have to speculate long for the British Invasion. It started off in the King's Road in London. In five years, Starbucks opened five new outlets every month. Today, British high streets are proud to announce they've been Starbuck-fucked 489 times.

If Starbucks advertised itself as an expensive fast-food and coffee takeaway, it would be fine, really. But the publicity driving it tries to make us believe that Starbucks is the love child of Italian coffee culture. This is selling a distorted vision of a three-century-old tradition all over the world and especially to countries with no café tradition, as those prove easiest to fool.

If you can stomach it, listen to Starbucks's CEO, Howard Schultz: 'Starbucks is based on a very intimate experience that takes place in a particular physical space, and, as a result of that, all of the signals that create the ambience, the romance, the theatre emotionally connect to the customer based on the intimacy of that relationship.'[6] If we were in 1789, his head would roll in a Parisian gutter for insult to reason.

It reminds me of Silvio Berlusconi, who, in February 2006, told the Italians that he was the Jesus Christ of Italian politics. Howard Schultz has the nerve to tell us, 'We, at Starbucks, are not in the coffee business serving people. We are in the people business serving coffee. We're not in the fastfood business. We

6. Quoted by John Carlin, the *Observer*, 13 July 2003.

really, sincerely, want to enhance people's lives.' Sounds like Schultz sees himself as the Jesus Christ of coffee culture.

Starbucks are coffee monsters, vampires of a civilisation of which they know nothing. I thought that as long as Starbucks only opened outlets in countries with no café tradition, we were safe – we could always flee and take shelter in Italy or France. How naïve of me.

The world fell apart in January 2004. Armageddon: the first Starbucks opened its doors in Paris, place de l'Opéra. Since then, its black-and-green shadow has spread over the *Ville Lumière*. Parisians love novelty, and brainwashed youth flock to wi-fi Starbucks. If they are stupid enough to abandon their heritage, well, let them. There is always Italy, unspoiled and untouched, at least as I write these lines.

Café society is not just about a few tables dotted on the pavement or froth on a caffè latte; it is a way of life, it is a place of public debate and discussion, it is a place for love and for fomenting revolutions. The French Revolution started off from the cafés in Palais Royal.

In the all-embracing café culture of Britain, I have finally found a few little gems that make for a better life. After much perambulation, I elected the few cafés where I could feel at home. They are former greasy spoons taken over by Italian families in the 1960s and 1970s, a British company with two outlets (Monmouth Coffee in Covent Garden and London Bridge), a small French grocery-café serving *madeleines* and whose waitresses address you by your first name while saying *vous*, and the Drunken Fish, a café created and managed by a young Canadian who knows all about conviviality. These cafés make up a perfect network of extended homes and familiar faces.

While Britain was taking up continental habits, France's café culture has been declining steadily, besieged by laziness and self-indulgence and, recently, weakened by the continuing onslaught of Starbucks and the like. Just imagine, in 1910, 42 million French people could choose from 510,000 cafés to get their daily fix. Today, 60,000 bistros cater for 58 million people. A lot of them deserved their demise: really bad coffee served by grumpy staff in smoky, dirty places. However, many decent cafés simply disappeared from towns and villages because people preferred to keep to themselves. Spending their evenings in front of the small screen rather than stepping outside to broaden their horizons. Other cafés have successfully reinvented themselves, attracting the young as well as more traditional customers. Some, in an ironic twist, have copied trendy New York and London eateries where international staff barely able to speak French ask you whether you want Chardonnay or Cabernet. A first: in France, one never defines wine in terms of variety of grape but only in terms of *terroir*, the soil where they grew. Oh, well, that's for another chapter.

Let's enjoy the last remaining years when, in Paris or London, the discerning café-goer can still elect his or her favourite joint. And to hell with Starbucks!

7

Classes

'I want changes to produce across the whole of this country a genuinely classless society so people can rise to whatever level from whatever level they started.' John Major in 1990

'The class war is over.' Tony Blair in 1999

'Just what Britain needs – an old Etonian hypocrite leading Her Majesty's Opposition. Just the thing to make the electorate less alienated from the political process – a Fettes vs. Eton old boys' match across the dispatch box for the next four years.' Stuart Jeffries in 2005

Another moment I have been dreading: writing about class in the UK. Along with sex – surely class must be the most risqué topic a Britain-based social commentator could tackle? And how *not* to? How *not* to talk about class warfare, snobbery and social prejudice after ten years living in the UK? It must be one of the trickiest subjects to handle, but, hey, just watch me jump in at the deep end. And give me a hand if I get out of breath; you wouldn't want to see a classless *gamine* go under, would you?

I never quite knew what class was until I set foot in England. No, I mean it, really. I honestly didn't know what it felt like, in practice and on a daily basis, not in theory like in my political science and sociology books. Let me explain; you can tick the boxes and see where you fit in. I grew up in what you would describe as a lower-middle-class part of Paris, neither posh nor dirty, just quiet and modest. My parents have been tenants since 1958. They are artists, thus dodging all-too-easy socio-economic categorisation. Both come from modest Breton families. They never went to university. My older brothers and I went to one of the best schools in the east of Paris, the closest to home, a Catholic school 'in association with the state'.

There are no religious schools as such in France; as I mentioned earlier, there is *l'école libre* – half-private, half-state schools with the same state curriculum for everybody except for an optional one-hour weekly session of Catholic studies. There are also expensive 100% private schools, but only failures and wealthy pupils go there. The most gifted go to free state schools, as they are usually the best. In France, on the whole, if it's good, it's free, and if it's free, it must be the best.

The primary and secondary school we went to in Paris accepted the best pupils regardless of their family income; half of them were given scholarships to cover the £300 annual fee. You didn't even have to be a Catholic. If you weren't, you just skipped the Catholic study class. My close circle of friends were the children of a concierge, an Ancien Régime aristocrat, a baker, a canteen chef, a policeman, a bank clerk, an MP, a road sweeper, a teacher, an accountant and a businessman. They were French; I now realise that some were atheist, Catholic, Jewish, and Muslim, of Spanish, Italian, Portuguese, Algerian, Tunisian, German, Vietnamese and West Indian origin. However, even in a Catholic school, we felt first and foremost French and, in general, sceptical about religion. You could worship Jesus in the privacy of your home, but you had to be discreet about it as, frankly, we all knew from what we had learned in our history lessons that all religions, especially Catholicism, were very dangerous. Inquisition, anyone?

We all spoke the same language, without any traces of class or regional accents. I only became aware of regional accents when we travelled to *la France profonde*. People from the countryside usually rolled their 'r's. The Marseillais certainly had a distinctive way of speaking, like the Belgians, the Swiss and the Quebeckers. I must emphasise that, at the time, there were no class accents. The working-class *titi Parisien* accent had disappeared by the 1980s, and the current suburban patois hadn't emerged yet. Nothing could distinguish my son-of-a-baker friend from my friend who was the son of well-known aristocrats: not the way they talked, the way they dressed, the words they used or their grammar, only their outlook on society and politics. *L'Ecole de la République* had done a good job. Respect.

That was then. Today, republican education shows worrying signs of fatigue. Seen from outside the classroom, it seems that political correctness and relativism, the new deity, have permeated the rigid egalitarianism of yesterday. If France feels more socially divided than it used to be when I was a teenager, it is also, I fear, a lot to do with the rise of *le culte de l'argent*, the cult of money, that is, as we'll see in a moment, so significant in the UK.

The challenge after passing *le bac* was to get into a free state preparatory class, the only measure of success. I was lucky and got into one to start preparing for the *grandes écoles*. From *le bac* onwards, my studies never cost my parents a penny; the State paid. *La République est bonne*. Going to L.S.E was a different story; it was so expensive (£3,000 a year) that I could only go if I got a scholarship. *Merci le British Council*. They paid my exorbitant fees and my rent. I also started working to help make ends meet, writing freelance for French dailies.

I grew up in a country where you could still feel the legacy of the revolution. The upper classes were not looked up to; no, the few of them left were ridiculed. I remember a dinner party in 2004 where the descendant of a miraculously spared lineage of French aristocracy was musing over the idea of asking the State to return one of the many châteaux his family had owned that had been annexed by the State after the revolution. Somebody at the table immediately snapped at him, saying, 'Don't you think you should simply be grateful to *la République* for being alive?'

Sure, along with a handful of aristocratic families, there were still real 'proles' left in the France of the 1980s: the last miners and factory workers. They smoked Gauloises, like my mum, went to cafés in the morning, drank *rouge* all the time, like my dad, and worked like dogs, just like both my parents. They'd be able to sing 'l'Internationale' and would continue to pay their Communist Party membership (before switching to Le Pen's National Front in 1986). The main difference between them and us was that they were communists, and we weren't. My father was a Gaullist, and my mum a socialist. I grew up in a country where at each general election, the Communist Party reaped 20% of the vote on average. Sounds strange to you, doesn't it? It even sounds weird to me now.

Apart from ideology, little separated *prolétaires* from people like us. For instance, in terms of income, the gap was small between factory workers and artists like my parents (except that, for the latter, there was always the possibility of suddenly earning much more). From 1945 on, culture and the arts had been made accessible to everyone. The State commissioned public oeuvres from great artists many of whom were often communists. For instance, in France, train stations, libraries, parks, town halls, etc. are adorned with the work of Fernand Léger and Picasso. In the theatre, the communist intellectuals and stars Jean Vilar and Gérard Philippe created the TNP (Théâtre National Populaire), making classics widely available to all. Going to see permanent collections in museums costs nothing, and the cinema barely more.

As for the bourgeoisie, a lot of it was still *éclairée*. 'Enlightened bourgeoisie', a nineteenth-century concept, referred to the cultured and self-educated (though often financially modest) class, which pushed through radical social reforms and sparked off revolutions, as in 1830. Some of the contemporary French bourgeoisie has somehow retained these attributes of the past. 'Bourgeois' is not a pejorative word in French and only becomes derogatory when attached to an adjective such as *borné*, meaning narrow-minded, *rétrograde*, meaning backward, or *petit*. The best French cinema shows the travails and successes of the bourgeoisie. Truffaut, Chabrol, Rohmer, Desplechin and Ozon have all filmed the many facets and attitudes of the bourgeois: in love, surrendering, discussing, arguing, cheating, murdering, rebelling and lying.

Today, I wouldn't claim that I grew up in a completely classless society. However, I did feel that apart from the very wealthy – we formed one nation with a common love for the good life and with firm ideals forged during the revolution. Our past hadn't all been glorious, oh no. But we could make amends for its failings. Everybody was welcome to join the party, and anyone who doesn't share the vision, go and get lost.

In the mid-1990s, upon my arrival in England, I discovered a country fascinated by aristocracy. This fascination seemed to generate two emotions: admiration and hatred, in equal measure. My (middle-class) English friends would defend the work of the Royal Family while loathing them at the same time. I could often sense their envy for the upper-class way of life, something to do with walking for hours in the mud and rain in wellington boots, and spending the weekend in a decrepit, cold stately home somewhere deep in the country. I could feel an admiration for upper-class sports, blood sports, sailing, riding and polo even though it was never articulated. I saw some of them shrinking in awe whenever they met members of the aristocracy; they'd unconsciously change the way they spoke. I saw Etonian acquaintances behaving rather strangely with working-class people, uttering expressions they'd never otherwise use. 'Cheers, mate', they'd say. I witnessed a profound uneasiness when relating to fellow countrymen from other social strata; it seemed much easier for them to talk to foreigners; they felt freer then, more natural, happier.

I discovered that social class revealed itself through the small details. First of all, the way you spoke and the words you used. I was amazed to learn that there were different nouns to name the same object, like 'settee', 'couch', 'sofa'. Which was used simply depended on social background. I was learning three languages at once, wonderful. Now for the way I talked: I sounded foreign on the whole, though apparently not French. 'Are you Swedish? German, perhaps?' cabbies used to ask. I didn't take it badly as I knew it was a compliment. But soon some of my friends (you know the type, upper-middle-class intellectuals who act like working-class thugs) reproached me for my accent, which had grown too posh for their tastes. Was I listening to too much Radio 4? In the end, they usually forgave me, as I remained first and foremost an alien, defying categorisation.

Details. I remember being told of the social difference in taste between strong ordinary tea, aka 'builders' tea' (PG Tips), and flavoured tea (Earl Grey, lapsang souchong, etc.): 'Don't serve Earl Grey to workers – they don't like it.'

However, what has been fascinating to observe in the last few years is not how socially self-conscious Britain is but rather how blurred social divisions have become. From the Burberry-clad chavs to the new forms of snobbery born at the fringes of the huge English middle class as each new tribe tries to define itself. We social commentators have had to play hide and seek with them to find our way through these new symbols, representations and chameleon attitudes.

In their report called 'Class 2004' Richard Benson and Alex

Milnes studied the increasing fragmentation of today's middle class.

The expansion of higher education, property ownership and service-sector employment has created a huge, economically powerful new class that is linked by a set of vague values. Its members tend to be ambitious, suspicious of authority, vaguely liberal and meritocratic and prone to judging people on the basis of birth, accent and profession. The new middle classes suffer from hubristic tendencies and a misplaced sense of entitlement. They watch their weight and think about their hairstyles. A lot. As such, they have created a very broad church.

But does this mean that we are moving towards a homogenous, more classless society? Not on your life. In the nation that George Orwell called the most class-ridden under the sun, the tendency towards snobbery and social codifications is so ingrained we just cannot give it up. As middle-class consumer choice has expanded, so we have been enthusiastically inventing new prejudices to separate ourselves into new consumer tribes, or mini-middle classes.

Money has proved one of the most fundamental agents of social evolution, social exclusion and snobbery. I'm not talking about the nouveaux riches of yesterday but of today's 'Haves' and 'Have Nots'. The Haves may be school drop-outs, and the Have Nots may be graduates with a PhD from Oxford. The Haves call the shots; they are the trendsetters; they say they love fashion, football, pop music and television while occupying the ground once belonging to the upper class. 'The new rich of the twenty-first century are beginning to look more like the plutocrats of the Edwardian era a century earlier, as they ostentatiously invade the territory of the old aristocracy, acquiring status and respectability while removing themselves from their own modest roots,' writes Anthony Sampson, in his ground-breaking book *Who Runs This Place?* They hardly share any common values, except for the love of money, which remains the only measure of fulfilment and success. They are the Beckhams and the City traders. The Have Nots may be penniless aristo-crats, educated but middle class with ambitions other than the purely material, or working-class people.

'The respect now shown for wealth and money-making has been the most fundamental change in Britain over four decades,' continues Anthony Sampson. 'The new élite is held together by a desire for personal enrichment, its acceptance of capitalism and the need for the profit motive, while the resistance to money values is much weaker and former anti-capitalists have been the people least inclined to criticise them once in power.'

This is where we go back to *le culte de l'argent* which I mentioned earlier. After 200 years of continuous social progress, are we now going backwards? After having fought social injustice, having humbled the rich, scared them with Socialism, Communism and taxation, we are now giving them everything back – lowering their taxes, opening the marketplace like never before so that they can play and speculate. Are we mad?

The good old class antagonisms will one day look almost desirable compared to the monstrous inequalities we are creating. The British will soon forget 1789. In a generation or two, our only memory of it may be as a new game for PlayStation: the X1789 revolutionary.

8

Death of the Independents

'**Independent:** free, autonomous, separate, sovereign.' *Oxford English Dictionary*

I spent my youth in the 12th arrondissement of Paris in the Nation district, a petit-bourgeois area, neither grand nor louche, just quiet. Take my arm; I will walk you down my old street. You know how we love food, don't you? Well, let's start our tour with, on the right, the pâtisserie where on Sundays my dad would sometimes get me a *mille-feuille*. I'd eat it later layer by layer in the most unorthodox manner.

At the *traiteur*, the delicatessen, just next to the pâtisserie, we would get a little *barquette* of *tarama* (taramasalata) and *céleri rémoulade* (celeriac in cream) as a Sunday treat. Next to the deli, a butcher, a luxury fruit and vegetable mini-market and a wine shop: too expensive, *on passe*. Another butcher. A few metres on, the fishmonger's, a particularly good address where a horde of apprentices rush about to serve the clients queuing chaotically on the pavement. Expensive too, but, hey, *ce n'est pas tous les jours dimanche!*[1]

Let's have a look across the street. There is yet another butcher, a *fromagerie*, a pâtisserie, a bakery, a café, a newsagent,

1. It isn't Sunday every day!

a Chinese delicatessen, an ironmonger's where I used to buy models of fighter planes to glue together to emulate my big brother, another fruit and vegetable stall and another café. From here, going up the street from the fishmonger's, we pass a wine shop, a pharmacy, a bakery, a ladies' footwear shop and a locksmith's.

Now let's cross rue Marsoulan, past the church on our right. Fewer stores, modern buildings from the 1970s and 'only' a florist, a coffee-roasting shop whose pungent smells permeated my childhood, a stationer's, a butcher, an Italian deli, two hairdressers, a wine shop, a mechanic's, the post office and a junk shop. Opposite, a little supermarket – Franprix – a bank, a bakery, a photo lab, a corset-maker, a café, a video outlet, a very old-fashioned clothes shop, a *librairie*,[2] a bric-à-brac shop and a beauty *salon* for self-conscious dogs. And here, sandwiched between dogs and books, is *chez moi*.

Here is a typical Parisian street; I dare say a typical French street. Since 1972, six out of the forty-one shops have changed. The old-fashioned clothes shop used to sell wine, but that change happened before I was four. The bookshop used to be a haberdashery selling ribbons and fabric by the metre, and in place of the video shop used to be a 'health' shop selling strange seeds and esoteric guides on how to live in harmony with nature. The corset-maker is about to close down, the newsagent has treated itself to a brand-new façade, and the pâtisserie at the top end has indulged in a new coat of *marron glacé* paint. In the thirty-odd years I have known this street, there have only been a few cosmetic changes and a slight gradual evolution in response to technological progress: the video is here for a short stay, fabric sold by the metre has gone, and the corset has died.

In 2006, out of these forty-one shops, you will find only one

---

2. Beware of the *faux-ami*: *librairie* is a bookshop not a library, which is a *bibliothèque*.

franchise: the supermarket, Franprix, a national chain. But you won't find a single subsidiary of an international chain: no Starbucks, no Zara, no McDonald's. Remember this . . . and now let's cross the Channel.

I mentioned earlier that when I first came to the UK, I roamed the streets of London in my search for the perfect café . . . and came across the Dôme, Pélican, Café Rouge, etc., British chains with a *soi-disant je ne sais quoi*. I dutifully checked them all out. My first experience was at the Dôme on Long Acre, Covent Garden. I sat and ordered a *café au lait*. The Swedish waitress replied, 'We only have *caffè latte*.' Oh? Fine. I had been told the Dôme cafés bought French newspapers every day, but the corner where they usually hung looked strangely empty. I asked where *Le Monde* had gone. The Australian manager told me that, because of the nuclear tests France was carrying out in the Pacific, he was boycotting French products (including news-papers). 'Don't you make your business from being, or at least looking, French?' I asked. He tutted, shrugged his shoulders and disappeared. At least, he'd got that bit right. The décor in those cafés felt like being on a 50s Hollywood set: endearing but totally fake. However, when I saw the same décor with the same posters reproduced in dozens of other cafés, I began to feel nauseated.

I rapidly developed an allergic reaction to chains. And that was before the Starbucks avalanche of September 1998. I intended, however, to persevere; and to find a decent independ-ent café in which I could feel at home. I eventually discovered a few former greasy-spoon caffs taken over by Italians decades earlier. There was Dino's off Mortimer Street, Italia Uno on Charlotte Street and Carlo's on the Farringdon Road. There was also Maison Berteaux on Greek Street, founded by an exiled Communard, the now defunct Café Java on Rupert Street, Café Brioche on West End Lane, the Blue Légume in Stoke New-ington and Café 206 on Westbourne Grove, where before it vanished Jeremy Paxman could be found before 8.30 a.m., always seated at the same table with an almond croissant, cappuccino and orange juice.

I was starting to spin my caffeine web in London; these independent cafés were the landmarks that grounded my existence.

Once you've had your *p'tit noir* in the morning, well, you need to buy bread, fruit, you know, the usual stuff. I was told to avoid fruit and vegetable stalls in the street or even little local markets, as the quality of their products didn't match that of supermarkets. What a shock for a French citizen: I was denied the pleasure of *faire le marché*; surely another Anglo-Saxon conspiracy?

For my psychological and emotional well-being, I really needed to find a string of local delis, butchers, fishmongers and wine shops. Not being surrounded by appetising food was proving to be a health hazard. Every day, I'd drown my sorrows and stuff myself with biscuits dipped in tea, and was putting on weight at an alarming rate.

The butchers nearby were either halal or far too expensive. I discovered two decent fishmongers, but needed to travel on the tube to get there; an hour's journey for a Dover sole. As for fruit and vegetables, forget it: they had no taste whatsoever, apart from English apples, a life-changing discovery. In the end, I gave up looking for magnificent and affordable independent trades shops; like everyone else I found myself shopping in standardised supermarkets and elected Waitrose as the best of the lot – the least awful – although excruciatingly expensive. I realised that only very wealthy people could afford to eat really well in the UK.

A few years later, when I found out about Borough Market, I wanted to build a shack under the arches and live there permanently; I couldn't wait for Fridays and Saturdays. Though the products were good (if pricey), it wasn't so much about buying food; it was the sheer animation, the cries of the vendors and the physical proximity of food that I had long been craving. In France, you grow up appreciating food with the eyes as much as with the taste buds; shop windows displaying heaps of fresh earthy products surround you almost everywhere you go. There is a familiarity, a connection with food that doesn't exist elsewhere in Europe, apart from, of course, in Italy, *nos frères de bouche*.

Books and stationery, another two loves of mine. Upon my arrival in London, I looked for bookshops. I don't mean charity shops selling books, second-hand bookshops or the bookshops specialised in old editions you find on Charing Cross Road, nor specialised stores like the theatre bookshop on Chalk Farm Road or at the National Theatre. I don't mean French bookshops. No, not even travel bookshops like the wonderful Daunt Books in Belsize Park and Marylebone or the W.H. Smith outlets, which only stock best-sellers. I mean a regular local bookshop selling new books and classics, a bookshop owned by a human being with passion, not by clueless employees of a large corporation. I found none. No, that's not true; I did know of one at Exmouth Market, London N1; it died within a year of my discovery. So I did the same as everybody else; I ordered books on Amazon and went to Waterstones. Not such a big deal, you might say, and of course you'd be right; it's fine. However, seeing every single independent retailer being swallowed by Big Bucks leaves a bitter-sweet aftertaste.

The same goes for stationery. The choice is between bland Ryman or beautiful and unaffordable Swedish Ordning & Reda, present only in exclusive parts of London. Where is the good old stationer's with scores of pens and notebooks to choose from? Dead and gone.

I know what you are going to tell me: it's all down to economics. Small independent shops are a luxury of the past. In order to survive today, they'd need to sell their goods at a higher price than the price-slashing mammoths of commerce. If they don't exist any more on British high streets, it is simply because the figures didn't add up and people were attracted by cheaper offers. You can't blame customers for wanting to pay less, can you? No, you can't. It is a fact of life. The market only rewards the strongest and the fittest, so off with the independent bookseller, off with the stationer, the butcher, the fishmonger, the craftsman, off with them all, off with little people with little ambition. Fine, but is this progress?

In France, the situation is quite different simply because the law protects independent shops in the city-centre from ruthless big corporations. The market has been bridled in order to safeguard a way of life, or so the Royer Act intended when it was passed on 27 December 1973. Since then, it has been very difficult for any retailer to open big stores in city centres, hence the mushrooming of *hypermarchés* and huge stores on the outskirts, creating monstrous shopping no-man's lands around French cities. In towns, small shops have survived longer than in countries where the market is king. However, the law, amended in 1996 by Chirac's ultra-liberal government, hasn't entirely prevented their decline, as today the insidious franchise has found its way onto French high streets.

We're told that French people today, like everybody else on the planet, increasingly prefer to visit the same shops all around the world. Do they really want to or are they *made* to believe that they do? Doesn't this sound exactly like the argument about TV programmes? 'We give rubbish to the people because that's what they want,' say hypocritical producers the world over. How insulting. We get bad TV programmes because producers, often educated at the best universities and business schools and who read high-brow stuff at the weekend in their country retreats, want to make a quick buck. They give us shit because shit is quick and easy to produce. Better programmes – i.e. entertaining and thought-provoking ones – take time to develop and produce. We, the public, watch crap because crap is all there is.

The Brits shop in franchised stores because there is no other choice, not necessarily because they prefer it. If they liked it so much, why would they flee as often as they can to countries like France, Italy, Spain, Portugal and Greece, where they marvel at a way of life that celebrates and preserves character, originality and authenticity?

Independent shopowners may have the nerve to charge higher prices than in supermarkets, they may not be always helpful, their choice of goods is not as wide as in a 10,000-square-metre store, but at least the majority of them are authentic, fresh and devoid of surreal commercial jargon. There is, for instance, no market-research behind the way they display goods in their windows; they just do it their way. Have you realised the real cost of the marketing blah-blah in every Starbucks's frappuccino? What the consumers buy is not only coffee, they also pay for the marketing geniuses who have succeeded in making them believe that their coffee is especially good, that the Starbucks ethos is about conviviality and friendship, that the place is cosy and the people making coffee know their stuff and actually care. What you're actually buying is froth, and froth can be expensive.

Sure, if you go and try out an independent shop, you never know the product's quality until you've tried it, whereas in a Gap store, be it in Tokyo, Kuala Lumpur, Geneva or Barcelona, you know exactly what you're going to get: the same crap all over the world.

Independence is not only a sum of figures, which do or don't add up economically, it's also intangible and uncountable, a spirit that is unique and cannot be faked. This is why chains go to so much effort to sell us that spirit. Deep down however, we know perfectly well that independence can neither be bought nor mass-produced.

It's the same old story in all trades, even in the movie business. There are the franchises, which work well when they are well produced, such as Working Title Films with Hugh Grant on the screen and Richard Curtis behind it. And then there are the independent films. A lot of these vanish before reaching the public for lack of luck, support, determination or talent, yet some of them, which nobody wanted to finance, reach us and are fêted by the people who have been longing to see them. What have they been desperate for? Something different, something unique. *Priscilla Queen of the Desert, East Is East, My Beautiful Launderette, the Full Monty, Girl with a Pearl Earring, My Big Fat Greek Wedding* and *Respiro* have all proved to be success stories against the odds.

It is always dangerous to want to mass-produce originality. All these films are one-offs, prototypes, impossible to copy. The same logic applies to shops: uniqueness cannot be reproduced. If it is, it is simply a con, a contradiction in terms. When Starbucks's boss, Howard Schultz, recalls how an espresso he had in a Milan café in 1983 changed his life, we stop and wait to hear what he has to say. He goes on to explain how Starbucks is in fact the love child of Italian café culture. Who does he think he's kidding? I wonder what went so terribly wrong between his first Italian love and the 'sock juice' we drink in our high streets today.

Let's go back to the street where I grew up, this ordinary haven of small enterprise, so far unspoilt by the jargon marketeers. Nothing remarkable here, no *folie des grandeurs* from a restaurateur who thinks he can duplicate his business all over the world, no stories of capitalist prowess, except perhaps the story of one café: Chez Prosper, owned by a young couple from the Auvergne. The café serves some of the best brands: Berthillon ice cream and Mariage Frères tea. It is loyal to traditional Parisian tableware with coffee cups once photographed by Brassaï in the 1930s, and the décor is original old ads and posters of the Tour de France. Only one breach in Parisian tradition: the fleet of *garçons* is helpful and charming. Open from 7 a.m. to 2 a.m., it serves decent bistro food non-stop with good little wines; nothing fancy and nothing too pricey. In the morning, from 7 a.m. to 8.30 a.m., a crowd of workers from nearby building sites have calva, as in calvados, with their coffee, standing at the counter alongside office clerks having their first caffeine fix on their way to work. After 9 a.m., it's the unemployed, artists, students and other leisurely customers who occupy the tables with a view on to the boulevard. From 12 to 3, it's the *coup de feu*, a very busy time with lunching office workers, then tea-time for grandmothers et al., followed by people having a drink on their way home from work or before going out, then dinner-time and late-night drinking till 2 a.m. All in all, a very socially diverse Parisian crowd.

Chez Prosper has proved so popular that their owners have bought another café, the former Café Notre Dame, opposite the cathedral, on the Left Bank. They transformed the old tourist trap into Chez Panis, a convivial Parisian café with an old-fashioned touch. Prices are inevitably higher than in not-so-trendy Nation. However, mixing with the occasional tourists, locals have come flooding back, electing Panis as their regular joint. Do the owners want to build a chain with their budding success? No, they don't. 'If we had cafés on every corner, it would depreciate their value. We would need a lot of investment from other partners and would therefore lose control. We are not a brand, we don't want to build an empire; we are just a family running a business. Our independence is not negotiable.'

9

Europe or Not Europe?

'We are simply asking to have our own money back.' Margaret Thatcher[1]

'Madam, you're not the only one!' François Mitterrand[2]

'The history of our involvement with Europe is one of opportunities lost,' said Tony Blair on 23 November 2001. That's what I'd call an understatement! If Britain had hopped on the Euro train after the Second World War, today it would be the toast of the town, *la crème de la crème*, the true master of Europe. Instead of joining forces with France and Germany, the English looked West, towards the unlikely cousins they both admire and look down on. All right, all right, it's not as simple as that. However, there is an element of truth in this simplistic view.

Churchill made a mistake. He may have dreaded the prospect of spending the rest of his life in bed with de Gaulle, who both infuriated and challenged him, but he should have known better:

1. At the European Summit in Dublin, 30 November 1979.
2. The matter still pending, François Mitterrand replies to Margaret Thatcher, who still wants her money back, at the European Summit of Stuttgart, on 19 June 1984. It famously led to a rebate being granted to Britain the same year.

Britain belongs in Europe. It is not an island off the coast of Nova Scotia. Besides, as we all know very well, New England couldn't give a damn about Old England. All North Americans see in the English is their quaint old charm, due mainly to their accent; nothing more, nothing less.

So France and Germany led the Euro pack from the beginning and, to this day, still do. It hasn't necessarily been a good thing: a triumvirate of Britain, France and Germany would have proved a more balanced and fairer leadership for a new and peaceful Europe. We could have avoided many of the misunderstandings and chagrins of the last fifty years.

After having failed to join us in our exciting, visionary idea of a united Europe, Britain finally reconsidered its position. But not out of love. Britain simply made a pass at Europe. After having tried many different economic options, Britain seemed at a loss as to how to put its economy back on the right track. So it thought after having tried everything else that maybe its lot would improve if it joined the EEC, a kind of desperate measure. Imagine a poor, handsome man telling a beautiful, rich girl, 'Hey, darling, wanna spend some time with me? Don't get me wrong; I don't love you, no, not at all, it's just that I thought I might be better off with you.' Charming. Well, I don't think de Gaulle had this analogy in mind when he chose to unilaterally veto Britain's application to join the EEC in 1963 and in 1967, but that's certainly what springs to my mind forty years on.

Britain never shared the vision of Europe as an idea and as an ideal worth fighting for. How can we blame Britain? First of all, how can we fail to understand that Britain didn't feel particularly enthusiastic about binding its future to that of ally (and old enemy) France, who shamefully let it down in 1940, let alone with that of ex foe twice over – Germany, who had bombed its cities into rubble. In this light, the idea of wanting to cuddle up to a real good friend, America, is perfectly understandable, if rather short-sighted.

For the English, there is no such thing as Europe, or Europa. Europa was the beautiful daughter of the King of Tyre (somewhere in today's Lebanon). Zeus, attracted by her great beauty, took the form of a white bull and lured her away from the Orient to the Western world, that is to say Crete. She later married the King of Crete and bore him a son, King Minos, who built the famous labyrinth . . . Yes, yes, I know what my English friends are going to say. This Greek myth sums it all up: Europe's great beauty, its predisposition to abuse, its labyrinthine ways, its bureaucracy and the ambiguity of its Eastern borders.

Why did de Gaulle reject Britain's application to the EEC twice? Hurt pride, I guess, having seen Britain's lack of faith in what to him was an indispensable plan for peace and stability on the Continent to end centuries of war and dispute. Then, suspicion: he saw Britain as the American Trojan horse in the European stable. His view was that Europe should offer a powerful and independent counterpoint to American and Soviet power. Today, the Cold War may be over, but the Gaullian idea of a robust Europe remains as pertinent as ever. But Britain's still not buying it. Shame.

Now that Europe has welcomed another ten new members, making the EU a community of twenty-five states, Franco-British rivalry is as fierce as it was when there were only seven of us round the table. Simon Hoggart sums it up very well in one of his sketches on Parliament's life:

All the questions about the EU are really about France, which could do with a good talking-to. There was a sad and affecting moment when Jack Straw was being told, in effect, that he had to grab France by the lapels and tell it to reform the CAP or he would not be answerable for what got chucked over their fence. 'I have talks all the time with our French colleagues. That's the easy part. The more difficult part is getting them to agree with our point of view.'[3]

'Getting them to agree with our point of view,' says Jack Straw. Sounds familiar – this is exactly what the French are trying to do to the English: convince them that their point of view is actually not such a bad one. So far, France and Britain have both failed. Just think of why the French voted *non* to the European Constitution. It is widely asserted – although the reality is more complex – that they said no because they thought that the Constitution would push Europe towards an Anglo-Saxon economic and social model – i.e. a free-market jungle in which social injustice is rife. Had the British voted, they most probably would have said no for exactly the opposite reason; that the European Constitution felt too French, with too much regulation. Has anybody read the text of the Constitution? It says nothing of the sort. Its most – and almost only – daring act was to create a European foreign minister. Now we can discuss the pros and cons of this particular point, but let's agree that, on both sides, myths and rumours rather than truth and facts fuelled the argument about the European Constitution.

The word 'constitution' frightens the English. I'll always remember President Valéry Giscard d'Estaing[4] being interviewed in English by BBC journalist Tim Sebastian on the TV programme *Hard Talk*.[5] Sebastian, for obvious reasons, kept asking the former French president about the exact nature of 'the spirit of the Constitution'. Giscard d'Estaing, seemingly uncomprehending, but smiling and gesticulating, said, 'But, but ze spee-reet, ze spee-reet eez everywhere!'[6]

3. The *Guardian* 2 November 2005.
4. The European Constitution was then being written under his authority.
5. On 14 November 2003.
6. But, but the spirit, the spirit is everywhere.'

Choosing the word 'constitution' was a faux pas. Giscard d'Estaing should have known better. The French, and continentals in general whose institutions derive from written Roman law, tend to forget that the British Constitution is unwritten. They also underestimate how much the English worship the supremacy of their Parliament, the cornerstone of the British way of life. Continentals also fail to remember that the English have been enjoying the stability of parliamentary democracy for much longer (three centuries!) than we, who are frequently driven to bloody revolution, restoration, *coups d'état*, fascism, communism, etc. Last but not least, Britain's *rupture* with the Catholic faith in 1530, and the creation of its own Church, have set it apart from the Continent. Indeed, the English have somehow relished the feeling of being different, detached from the Continent. It made them feel special, superior even. The French, however, tend to think that the English are not so different. So we, the French, don't understand each time they reject Europe – i.e. us and our vision. It annoys us, but it shouldn't: it makes perfect sense.

When I talk about myths and rumours surrounding Europe, I should really talk about misinformation. The English are totally and thoroughly lied to about Europe. The Murdoch press is one of the culprits in this evil game. In Britain, belligerent columnists rant day and night about Europe, Brussels and Eurocrats, and say the most ludicrous things. One of hundreds, Melanie Phillips's column in the *Daily Mail* is preposterously partisan. The style is always the same: right-wing-tabloid-pamphlet bullying. Blows below the belt are welcome. So much for the legendary English fair play.

To give you an example, if the EU Constitution had been adopted, 'Member states would have been left with little more power than a heritage theme park,' says Phillips. 'Moreover, this was to be a virtual-reality state, a free-floating entity with no political, legal or cultural anchorage and created instead entirely by bureaucratic legerdemain.' She then rants on about the European commissioners' 'monumental arrogance' for believing that the concept of Europe is indeed meaningful. 'People owe their allegiance to their own country, because they are part of a community of people shaped by common laws, history, customs, religion and culture. Because of this attachment, people will die for their country. No one would ever die for the EU.' How can she be so sure? Did the International Brigades (who weren't all communists and who didn't hesitate to fight alongside Spanish republicans in 1936) feel this way? Did the British feel that way when France was invaded by Germany? Luckily, they didn't. They died for their friends across the Channel. A lot of people would die for their neighbours and friends even if they don't speak the same language. 'But then, who can be surprised at such arrogance when it was Herr Verheugen[7] who presented a copy of the EU Constitution to an Italian astronaut to take to the International Space Station – presumably to demonstrate that its cosmic appeal should also colonise outer space.' Aha. Phillips, like almost all her colleagues, is paid for undermining the actions and speech of anybody with a funny accent speaking well of Europe by way of derision, sometimes calumny.

Often the misinformation is more subtle, just made of creeping insinuations. Again, the *Daily Mail* provides the more colourful examples of Europhobic ranting. We can read, for instance, that Britain is facing an HIV epidemic . . . due to EU enlargement! 'Shocking new figures are likely to reignite fears that Britain may be at risk from an infectious diseases epidemic now that Europe has expanded.'[8] As for the EU Commission, it is simply said to be 'up to its neck in corruption [. . .] The European Parliament is notable mainly for the padded expenses

7. Vice-president of the EU Commission.
8. Zoe Bolton, the *Daily Mail*, 11 November 2004.

of MEPs.'[9] It is well known that European MPs spend their days devising strategies by which to rob British taxpayers of their money. As if they had nothing else to do.

The evils of this endemic misinformation in Britain could have been reversed if Tony Blair had seized the opportunity of the 2001 general election and tied it up with a referendum about Europe (and the euro). If he had put all his weight behind it and used his famous powers of persuasion and spin to convince the British people that enough was enough and that Britain belonged in Europe then we wouldn't be facing any of today's deadlocks. Iraq has now made it almost impossible for the British to believe whatever Blair has to say, especially in the domain of foreign policy. Besides, Iraq has demonstrated the outrageous hold American neo-cons and Murdoch have on the British Prime Minister. For the neo-cons, a strong Europe is a threat to American hegemony. And wasn't it Rupert Murdoch who publicly complained of Britain's 'appeasement' towards France? If Blair was sincere when he said that he wanted Britain to be 'a bridge between Europe and America', then he's failed terribly.

What has the British presidency of the EU achieved in 2005? Well – apart from the question of Turkey's admission to the EU, not much. And why so? Maybe because Blair and New Labour don't agree on Europe any more. As commentator Jackie Ashley rightly puts it:

In June, when the European Constitution was wrecked by French and Dutch voters, the Prime Minister, holding the rotating presidency of the EU, announced a pause for reflection. Recently, there has been a mutter round the Continent – nearly four months of silence is a long time for a pause: it is now time for the British to suggest what should happen next. But the silence comes not merely from the complexity of the

9. The *Daily Mail*, 28 May 2005.

European challenges (the budget, Turkey, trade, agriculture) but also from a serious division inside Britain's Labour family about what Europe is for [. . .] On the one side is the familiar centre-left case that the EU exists to protect its citizens against the pain of globalisation. This is the case Robin Cook made so eloquently for years. On the other is the claim that the old vision of an integrated social Europe is now bust, and the challenge is to embrace open markets, not raise walls. This is the case coming from the Brownites as much as Downing Street.[10]

What a gloomy picture. Yet how could Blair lack courage on Europe when every day his fellow countrymen vote with their feet! Facts and figures: 100,000 Britons have permanently settled in France, and more than 600,000 of them now own a property there where they live part-time.

Officially, there are 151,000 second homes in England and Wales, but they come a poor second to property owned abroad. The industry estimates that there are 750,000 homes in Spain owned by British nationals, roughly 600,000 in France and many more in places such as Portugal, Mediterranean countries other than Spain and, increasingly, Eastern Europe. So at least 1.5 million British households – roughly 6% of the total – have given up sufficiently on their 'normal' lives to want to live somewhere else half the time. And that is just those who can afford it.[11]

France's national statistics office, INSEE, revealed in January 2005 that the full-time British population in France as a year-on-year percentage increase is now growing faster than the Maghreb communities: 46% for Brits compared with 15% for

10. The *Guardian*, 24 October 2005.
11. David Nicholson-Lord, the *New Statesman*, 2 August 2004.

North Africans. The second largest percentage growth is of immigrants from the new EU member countries.

Given that emigration is supposedly associated with economic failure and that New Labour keeps telling us how successful Britain has become, one wonders what lies behind the British exodus to the Continent? Wouldn't it be 'better quality of life'? Hmm, we may have touched a nerve here. Britain may be 'working', but are the British happy? 'Operational' doesn't necessarily mean healthy. Could it be that a good health service, good public transport and the social advantages found in continental Europe have played a part in the British émigrés' decision to leave Britain? But then, all this – a good health service, good public transport and social advantages – doesn't just happen by chance. They exist because the taxpayers' money has been well spent, because there is a mutual agreement between the State and its people on what is important. Could it be that what the British actually want is more State? Blair, are you listening? But, no, surely, I must be mistaken . . .

One could argue that the British are really just cynical pragmatists. If they have a bit of dough, they invest it in a place in the sun, preferably where food is good, life nice and public services impeccable. If they flock to continental Europe, it's nothing to do with feeling European. However, I'm not buying it. By emigrating to continental Europe more today than ever before, the Brits show, perhaps unconsciously, that they've moved a long way from their stalwart isolationism and understand the European reality. It doesn't mean, however, that they're ready to give MEPs more power. They're still too attached to the supremacy of Parliament to even contemplate yielding political power. Nonetheless, I insist that cheap housing on the Continent and low-cost airlines are doing more for the English than just another good investment.

10

Gentlemen or Thugs

'**Thug:** a brutal ruffian or assassin. From Hindi "thag", literally "thief", from Sanskrit "sthaga", "rogue".' *Oxford English Dictionary*

'**Gentleman:** a man of good or noble family, an aristocrat; a well-bred man.' *Oxford English Dictionary*

Sorry if the following sounds rather arcane and my thoughts appear somewhat fuzzy. This chapter is based more on instinct and gut feeling than on facts and figures. Besides, I'm venturing into the delicate subject of British men. Needless to say, I have not met every single one of them; my reflections are based only on the close encounters I have had with a few of them and on the careful observation of numerous others. So, whenever I refer to *l'homme anglais*, you must understand that I'm only talking about those whose paths I have crossed, ranging from Richard – a printer's apprentice I met on a language course and who was to be my first romance at the age of fourteen – to Prime Minister Tony Blair.[1]

---

1. Whom I haven't studied as closely personally. I met Tony Blair once, in Downing Street, when Prime Minister Dominique de Villepin was visiting in July 2005.

I wouldn't dream of trying to paint a universal portrait of *Homo Britannicus*, for this species is far too diverse. I usually find it more useful to analyse individuals' behaviour through their psychological make-up, rather than by way of their nationality. Nationality and gender are two rather misleading profiling tools. However, the culture one has been brought up in leaves marks, like footprints in wet cement. We are composed of many strata, and culture is one of them.

When I think about British men, there is one thing I find they often share and that has always intrigued me. I haven't thoroughly analysed or researched these impressions and fleeting memories. So far, I have chosen to leave them unexamined, like a mystery that doesn't yet need solving.

'It', the essence of British maleness, is that there is something very physical and violent about British men. I'm not talking about domestic violence but about something rather more abstract – a restrained violence, an inner tension.

The restrained physical force I'm trying to describe is not machismo in the Latin sense of the word. Machismo on the Continent often sounds and looks like a choreography of words and body language, outwardly expressed to impress women and defeat potential rivals. Latin machismo also displays superiority over women. In that sense, one can argue that Latin machismo exists essentially in relation to the opposite sex. The physicality of British maleness, however, seems to permeate British culture as a whole.

Is it acquired very early on in life, taught and absorbed at school from a very young age? Is it true that sport and physical activities have a more predominant place in the UK than in France? Absolutely right, they do. *La culture physique*, as we call it in France, has not, in the last fifty years, been as widely developed in French schools as in Britain. The focus in the French education system has always been to value *culture générale* over practical and physical studies.

In the 1980s, sport for me was a two-hour session a week, consisting of running for an hour round the same bloody circuit and doing 'gym' on smelly mattresses. Brains were the place where the real action took place. And, God, how we sweat. Have a look at French male intellectuals of the last fifty years: few have anything approaching the physique of an athlete. They are chain-smokers, nail-biters, surviving on books and black coffee, wearing a perpetual frown. They almost all look gaunt, in desperate need of fresh air and a good work-out at the local gym. All right, this sounds a bit over the top, but, please, visit a few cafés in Paris; you'll find them there, looking the same whether they are twenty or sixty. Only one of them must be going to the gym: BHL, aka Bernard Henri Lévy. He has worn a dazzling white shirt open from neck to navel and long black curls down to his shoulders since 1968. Camus was fit too, but he played football.

British intellectuals are more difficult to spot. They don't have a home they can go to every morning: café society is too recent to have played the same nurturing role as in France. British intellectuals often hide behind the smoke screen of their jobs, whether in academia, journalism, publishing or science. When you eventually track them down, it is surprising to see how seriously they take their physicality. Body and brain seem to cohabit harmoniously. For many, sport has had as important a place in their education as mathematics or going to the cinema. In Britain, a pupil who is good at any given sport enjoys the admiration of his peers; he or she is respected. In France, they are considered at best an eccentric, at worst a retard.

I'm talking here about prejudices, not infrastructure. For instance, you'll find more Olympic-size swimming pools in Paris than in the whole of Britain. France boasts a few great athletes, who regularly reap their share of medals at world and Olympic competitions. The State has done its job in providing aspiring champions with the tools they need to perfect their art.

However, *sportifs*, or anybody who exercises, are usually held in affectionate contempt. It's like intellectualism in Britain: in France, one must pretend not to do it. If you exercise, claim it is *pour le plaisir*.

Sport in Britain also fulfils a very important social role. No wonder modern sport emerged in Britain in the eighteenth century parallel to the affirmation of parliamentary sovereignty. They both participated in the creation of specific places where violent class conflict could be contained and transcended. Achievement in sport has always been highly regarded by all classes of society and has helped erase social boundaries. Of course there are so-called 'gentlemen's sports' such as rugby and cricket and 'thugs' sports such as football, yet an athlete is a potential winner and winning is what really counts. On the sports field, so-called gentlemen and so-called thugs are competitors together. There even seems to be a mirror effect in which ruffians look up to aristocrats and gentlemen wish they were thugs.

Violence and physical activities have bound these two extremities of society together for centuries. Noblemen who went to war would prepare through sport of all types. When they lost the monopoly on war, they carried on practising 'blood sports', such as hunting or duelling, as well as all sorts of strenuous outdoor activities, as a way of keeping alive their ancestors' legacy. As for thugs, they have practised street war, with its own share of violence, and murder. In France, it's difficult to find common ground between thugs and *gentilhommes* – perhaps because the revolution has left too few aristocrats.

The mutual fascination between 'gentlemen' and 'thugs' can also be illustrated by the use of language. I have met so many upper-middle-class men borrowing the manners, accent and language of working-class yobs. Director Stephen Frears tells the story of how he first met actor Daniel Day-Lewis. Frears was auditioning for the leading parts of *Prick Up Your Ears*. We are in 1982 and twenty-five-year-old 'Daniel Day-Lewis arrives and talks with a very strong working-class accent; all his behaviour is that of a thug. He then tells me he is the son of Cecil Day-Lewis, Poet Laureate. Why, I wonder, does he feel he has to hide his sophisticated personality under such a violent mask?'

In Britain, violence is expressed through its language. Some words are so powerful and their connotation so shocking that they cannot be printed or uttered on television. I don't even know whether I can write them here. The words 'fuck' and 'cunt', for instance, carry with them an incredible force, which hasn't diluted with time. When Ken Loach's film *Sweet Sixteen* got a Certificate 18 in Britain because of its 'strong language', preventing a young audience – for whom the film had been written – from seeing it, the French were simply dumbfounded. In France, words such as *putain* and *con* have lost all their power to shock; their true meaning is even lost on most people as they've come to seem like mere punctuation marks with which you spice up your speech. The Marquis de Sade used these words so extensively in his books that soon by the beginning of the eighteenth century they were no longer taboo. A *con*, the exact translation of cunt, is used by everybody in France to say imbecile. *Con, conne, connard, connerie* are mild words today in the French language.

More importantly, in France, swearing and the use of strong language are often an integral part of verbal interaction. Such words are heard frequently on the social scene and, due to the theatricality of the French language, their potency is lessened. This doesn't mean words are not important; they are, but they're just part of a show. This drastically reduces their power to shock. Besides, insulting and being insulted in France is not such a big deal; like bitching about everything, it's a national pastime. However, in Britain, a much more polite society by nature than France, swearing, cursing and insulting retain potency, a real taboo-breaking experience. 'Gentlemen' and 'thugs' like using swear words for the same reason: the implied violence, the social transgression, the thrill of shocking the other.

Finally, bullying seems to me yet another way of illustrating this much-contained violence of British men. Tragic stories of pupils committing suicide after having been the victims of bullies at school regularly make gruesome headlines in the British press. Bullying in offices, the army and even at the BBC is an issue often addressed and discussed in the British media. There is no exact word to translate 'bullying' in French. We talk about intimidation, but the concept of bullying seems specific to Britain. It seems to be linked to the physicality of domination. Bullies will behave in a domineering manner until their victim surrenders. There is very little talk about bullying or any equivalent in French schools as related by the French media. In *le monde du travail*, people complain of harassment, stress and intimidation but not of bullying. Direct confrontational style being a permanent feature in French society, tension is usually released verbally, thus reducing the force behind the uppercut.

11

Hugh Grant

'Bashing the British film industry has long been a national pastime, along with moaning about the weather and worrying about the sex lives of politicians.' Mark Kermode, film critic[1]

'All I can say is: come friendly bombs and fall on our native film industry now.' Peter Bradshaw, film critic[2]

'There are ten intertwined stories in *Love Actually*, and almost all of them involve stiff, inarticulate, indecisive middle-class British men who are cured of their condition by foreign or lower-class women. If that's your fantasy, then seeing it acted out by the likes of Hugh Grant and Alan Rickman, against a Christmassy backdrop, will be heavenly.' Steve Rose, film critic[3]

At the junction of New North Road and Poole Street in North London stands the ghost of the Gainsborough Studios. In 2002, I walked down the little alley and along the canal, where the young Alfred Hitchcock had trod so often in the early 1920s. Seagulls wheeled and squawked above me as I passed the Crown

1. The *Guardian*, 10 October 2004.
2. The *Guardian*, 25 November 2005.
3. The *Guardian*, 19 March 2004.

and Manor Boys' Club and followed a path in the shadow of the famous chimney, proud symbol of the bygone studios. I was there to write a report and to reminisce. The Gainsborough Studios were about to be turned into a complex of lofts and shops for trendy, wealthy City traders.

Every film-lover remembers the Gainsborough's emblem: a woman's profile, that of actress Sarah Siddons, wearing lace, as if painted by Gainsborough himself. This image, along with the man striking the gong from Rank and MGM's roaring lion, has shaped the history of cinema.

In 1919, Jesse Lasky bought the former power station from the Metropolitan Line and kept the building as it was, with its disproportionately large chimney. He went on to buy state-of-the-art movie equipment and transformed the place into a film studio. Five years later, the twenty-eight-year-old film distributor Michael Balcon took over. He decided to promote a chubby twenty-year-old caption writer to assistant director; his name was Alfred Hitchcock. In 1926, Alfred directed his first 'truly Hitchcockian' feature, *The Lodger*, starring heart-throb Ivor Novello. The storyline: a landlord suspects that his lodger may be Jack the Ripper. Hitchcock wanted to leave the ending open, with Novello walking away into the night, leaving the audience uncertain as to whether he really was the monstrous murderer. Balcon didn't want to take risks; Novello was too big a star to be cast as a murderer. Cinemas would no doubt be burned down by angry mobs! The lodger's innocence had to be proved at the end of the film. Hitchcock gave in.

Remember Ivor Novello? The Rudolph Valentino from Wales, the John Barrymore with a cockney accent! Today, the Ivor Novello Appreciation Bureau still keeps his cult alive. Cinema is the youngest of the arts – only 110 years old, one exceptional human lifetime. Ivor Novello and Brad Pitt are separated by mere seconds on the timeline of culture and the arts.

In Britain, when commentators and professionals talk about British cinema, they talk about its crisis or impending death. They usually tell you so in hushed tones, looking over their shoulders, as if there were a conspiracy brewing in a nearby office in Soho or Westminster. There are few subjects in Britain today that produce such pessimistic, schizophrenic behaviour. It's as if they have all turned French overnight, speaking incessantly about *la crise*, except this time it's *la crise du cinéma britannique*.

If there is a crisis in British cinema, it's all down to a problem of memory: loss of memory on a national scale. I must first hit where it hurts most: in my own field, that of film critics, those supposed *passeurs* of knowledge. When I first arrived in Britain, I was curious to see whether distinctive British film criticism existed, a really different way of looking at films. I read all the film-review sections of magazines, broadsheets, tabloids and specialised revues; I was bewildered. The majority of film critics that I read didn't know what they were talking about and, even worse, didn't seem to care. The reviews often read as if their authors had knocked out the 500- or 1,000-word pieces in a jiffy, between their fourth gin and tonic at the Groucho Club and their first pint in the pub. Their argument for liking a film seemed to read more or less as a) the leading actress is sexy; b) the locations are cool; c) the pace is fast with great action scenes. Their references? Dating back to the 1980s for the most knowledgeable of them, and we're talking exclusively about films made in the English language. In their book, foreign films, as in films made in all languages other than English, are by definition 'difficult' and 'specialised' for an 'art-house audience'. For the majority of these critics, *Citizen Kane* is not a great masterpiece, Ingmar Bergman is a bore, Woody Allen a loser, Jean-Luc Godard a retard, Fellini grotesque and Eisenstein, er, who? These are the guys who are supposed to make us want to leap to our feet and run to the nearest cinema to see the next unmissable film.

I soon discovered that some of them were doing film reviews *faute de mieux*, between better assignments. Better assignments! I couldn't believe it. The cultural divide widened each time I opened a newspaper at the film section. I remember the day I discovered the name of the new film critic of a tabloid. They had thought no better than to ask a 'celebrity', a popular writer who had just revealed his past drug addiction in an autobiography or had been on *Big Brother*, can't remember which. I saw him at a screening, his legs wide apart, slouching over two seats, beer in hand, jeering throughout the film. He was actually having a good time; he had even brought some of his mates with him. The film was about football hooligans. They left a sea of empty cans behind them.

Of course, there are *real* film critics in Britain, but unfortunately they either write for exclusive revues or have become blasé, unable to muster the slightest enthusiasm for a film that requires all their powers of persuasion to make people want to go and see it. Even worse, they often have a very low opinion of themselves, their work and British cinema as a whole.

There couldn't be a starker contrast with France. There, one has to kill to become a film critic; there is no more highly regarded position in a newspaper than film critic (or political editor). You think I'm kidding? Think again. To understand the place of *cinéma* in French culture, just go to Paris, take the Métro at any time of the day and listen to your fellow passengers. They will often speak about the latest film they saw (at the cinema, that is, not on DVD), about how it was written, directed, acted, photographed even. These people are bank clerks, students, pensioners, young mothers, anybody and everybody. *Cinéphilie*, as in the love of cinema, is not an élitist pastime in France; it is an existential passion.

Let's try to get a broader picture. If *cinéma* occupies such an important place in France, it's only because culture, as in the arts, is regarded as being of national importance. Of strategic importance even. A film, as any other work of art, conveys a way of observing the world and interpreting it. A country's culture is like its naval fleet.

When I started my PhD at the London School of Economics, I wanted to study the cultural relationship between France and Britain during the Belle Epoque (1890s–1914). I kept repeating the word 'culture' to my supervisor, but he didn't seem to understand. It took me six months to explain that I wanted to study the influence of the arts and ideas on international politics of the time. He looked surprised. What a strange idea. Surely economics lead the world, not ideas and certainly not the arts? In Britain, the Queen bestows OBEs and other royal accolades on people who have sold a lot of records, made lots of money in films and created box-office bonanzas for the country, but not on great artists or great intellectuals. I could see why he was surprised.

Over the first few months after my arrival in England, I observed the people in government: no Ministry for Culture. I thought everything would change with Tony Blair. Yet, even after May 1997, no Ministry for Culture per se, just a department in charge of media, sport, arts, heritage, tourism and the National Lottery. I then realised the meaning of the expression 'Ministry of Fun'. Still, better than nothing, I thought. I looked for the position of its minister within the government; my eyes kept going down and down the list. I met and interviewed him: Chris Smith. He was obviously biding his time, waiting, like most film critics in Britain, for a better appointment. In France, the minister for culture is a much fought-over job, position number four in the government, with a huge portfolio and budget.

Culture and the arts only seem to be of interest to the British government *if* and *when* they start pouring money into the Treasury coffers. As for subsidising the arts in Britain, most politicians would rather not have to do it, but, hey, there are still a few liberals in the theatre and academic circles who might scream a bit too loudly if nothing came their way. Subsidies are thus an unavoidable burden that is left for the Arts Council to bear. In France, subsidising the arts is an honour and a national duty. As I said earlier, taxpayers pay handsomely for their artists' survival, and artists and all employees of the cultural sector can take advantage of a unique tailor-made benefit system. The system has been designed so that aspiring actors, directors, producers and screenwriters don't have to accept odd jobs to make ends meet. Sounds crazy to you, doesn't it? Sounds like one of the many luxuries France will have to give up in order to reduce her huge debts. Maybe.

So I simply had to come to terms with the fact that cinema, like everything else cultural in Britain, wasn't taken seriously, at least not in public. There are, of course, serious art- and film-lovers in the UK, but they seem to have to hide, like the early Christians in pagan Rome.

There is no denying that cinema is an industry manufacturing entertainment products, and celebrities, by the dozen, who go on to market international brands. It has almost always done that, but the point is that cinema is diverse and that Britain has been among the best at certain genres. Just remember.

British cinema has given the world some of the most vibrant films ever made. Let us go back to the Gainsborough Studios where soon Boris Karloff, Margaret Lockwood, Gracie Fields, Jack Warner, Michael Redgrave, Richard Attenborough, Stewart Granger and James Mason joined the young Alfred Hitchcock on the benches of the canteen. In 1938, *The Lady Vanishes* made a star of the elegant Michael Redgrave. A few years later, James Mason and Stewart Granger shared the limelight in *Fanny by Gaslight* by Anthony Asquith. The Ealing comedies made the world laugh,[4] while Carol Reed with *Odd Man Out, Outcast in*

---

4. To name but a few: *The Lavender Hill Mob, The Man in the White Suit, Kind Hearts and Coronets, Whisky Galore, The Ladykillers, Father Brown*, etc.

the Islands, *The Fallen Idol* and *The Third Man* and Michael Powell's films such as *The Edge of the World*, *A Matter of Life and Death*, *The Red Shoes* and *Peeping Tom* made us dream and forced us to the edge of our seats.

Later, British cinema would make the world stop, look and listen. Free cinema, heralded by Lindsay Anderson, Karel Reisz and Tony Richardson, proved as raw and revolutionary as the French New Wave. Through them, cinema showed the real face of Britain, not just selected parts of it. They exercised no restraint in the way they filmed or talked about a subject; they freed cinema from all previous references and mannerisms. Their films were streams of indomitable consciousness. Made with little money and sustained by the filmmakers' energy, they thrilled generations of movie buffs who had never before seen anything so real on screen. Remember Tony Richardson's *A Taste of Honey* and *The Loneliness of the Long Distance Runner*, Lindsay Anderson's *This Sporting Life*, Karel Reisz's *Saturday Night and Sunday Morning*, John Schlesinger's *Billy Liar* and Jack Clayton's *Room at the Top* and *The Pumpkin Eater?*

The world was so eager to share this exuberant energy that filmmakers came rushing to London to make films there: Roman Polanski made *Repulsion* in 1965 and *Cul-de-Sac* the following year; Truffaut directed *Fahrenheit 451* that same year; and so did Michelangelo Antonioni with *Blow-Up*. In 1968, Stanley Kubrick settled in the UK for good after making *2001: A Space Odyssey* and *A Clockwork Orange*. Need I go on?

At that time, yet a new generation of British filmmakers were already focusing their lenses, perfecting their vision. Among them were Terence Davies, Ken Loach, Stephen Frears and Mike Leigh – four different personalities and four distinctive voices, the pride of Britain. Don't cringe over that expression; embrace it and be proud. Some of these new talents started in television before making their debut on the big screen. All retained their uniquely British voices, ones that Hollywood could never have tamed.

When Hugh Hudson and Colin Welland went to collect their Oscars in Los Angeles in 1982 for *Chariots of Fire*, their famous words – 'The Brits are coming' – created one of the most embarrassing misunderstandings. Their American *succès du jour* tainted British cinema for a long time. Many British producers and financiers became convinced that Britain had to provide exclusively picture-postcard films for an international audience in order to get Oscars – in their eyes, the only measure of success. This became an ideology, the same one adhered to today by executives at the UK Film Council, the national body whose job it is to help 'nurture home talent'. The mere idea that British films could be successful at home became preposterous; suddenly, British cinema needed America's stamp of approval and savoir faire above all. But why? How could British filmmakers suddenly forget how great they were? Why think only Hollywood could make great box-office hits? Why mimic the Americans? How deeply insecure to doubt one's ability so much. Do the Italians think Hungarians make better pasta?

The only thing this nefarious ideology achieved was to cause conflict between members of the same family. There were suddenly only two species of British filmmaker: the money-makers and the money-losers. Working Title Films, often starring Hugh Grant and written by Richard Curtis, set the standard for impeccably well-wrapped fantasies for an 'international' audience that make billions at the box office worldwide, while the original voices of British cinema, featuring the real and magnificent Britain, are struggling to survive with little or no subsidies. Ironically, they owe their existence to foreign film festivals and the community of world cinephiles. Fêted abroad and looked down on in their own country. How can you explain that the great Terence Davies hasn't made a film since his masterly *House of Mirth* in 2000? And if Ken Loach, Mike Leigh and Stephen Frears still make films, it's mainly thanks to European financiers, not British.

Since the 1990s, a new generation has emerged whose talent has had difficulty blossoming in this environment of ignorance, a pernicious ideology, self-doubt and a lack of financial and moral support. Nevertheless, they have produced inspired work: Emily Young, Sarah Gavron, Lynne Ramsay, Shane Meadows, Pawel Pawlikowski, Thomas Clay and Josh Appignanesi to name but a few. The most important thing is, watching their films, you realise that, in their eyes, Ivor Novello will never grow old.

12

Journalism

'Our Republic and its press will rise or fall together. An able, disinterested, public-spirited press, with trained intelligence to know the right and courage to do it, can preserve that public virtue without which popular government is a sham and a mockery. A cynical, mercenary, demagogic press will produce in time a people as base as itself.' Joseph Pulitzer[1]

'Swan Bake – asylum seekers steal the Queen's birds for barbecues [. . .] Callous asylum seekers are barbecuing the Queen's swans. East European poachers lure the protected royal birds into baited traps, an official Metropolitan Police report says.' The Sun[2]

When my mother recalls how, as a small child with her parents during the darkest hours of the German occupation, they received echoes of the Free World, their ears glued to the *poste de radio* in the cellar of the house so as not to reveal their contentious activities to the outside world, I measure the

1. In May 1904, writing in *The North American Review* in support of his proposal for the founding of a school of journalism.
2. Printed on the front page on 4 July 2003. It was pure invention, which the paper later had to admit.

emotional and historical importance of those three letters, BBC, which came to embody the courage of a nation and freedom of the press the world over. Sixty years later, the memory, handed down from generation to generation, feels as intense as ever.

In the 1980s, I grew up thinking that France had an average press with a few good journalists and that in Britain there stood the *indépassable* BBC while the tabloids lay in the gutter. The French, having been so far immune to the tabloid-press cannot understand how the best in journalism – the BBC – could cohabit with what they see as journalistic muck. And so I arrived in England with reservations about the state of the British press.

It took me some time to look at a tabloid, let alone actually buy one and read it. Their front pages had a hypnotic effect on me. First of all, there was the naked flesh splashed all over them to provoke passers-by. I couldn't help but stop and stare. Not in awe but in disbelief, like when you're at a zoo and you see an animal for the first time. Then there were the gigantic headlines; I wondered if they weren't actually eye tests. It took me a long immersion in the country's popular culture and language to make sense of their often crass but witty wordplays. When I got to the stage of actually buying a tabloid, opening its pages and reading the articles, my brain would melt. I tried to reassure myself; surely these were marginal publications read by a few eccentrics? Then I discovered the readership – 9 million copies sold daily – a sharp decline from the 13 million a day sold in the 1960s; I had a panic attack. Should I pack my bags, rush to the Eurostar and leave this madhouse of a country? But Britain is one of the greatest democracies in the world. It must have its reasons for harbouring such a cheap and nasty press. I decided to stay, but I lived through a few long months of denial, pretending tabloids didn't exist. You see, at the beginning, I was madly in love with Britain and the British. In my eyes, there was nothing they could do wrong; their occasional quirks were always admirable, ipso facto, tabloids just couldn't exist.

As time went by with my new-found objective appreciation of the British, I was able to digest a tabloid along with my daily diet of different broadsheets. Then I became a journalist myself. Begin the cross-examination.

With the LSE standing at the end of Fleet Street, I immediately ventured into the *quartier* where I was told all newspaper people had worked, gossiped and boozed for two centuries. I scrutinised the façades, the pubs with their little alleyways and secret passages. Then I went to see Canary Wharf, where several newspapers had relocated. What a stark contrast: from nineteenth-century family capitalism to modern global power, while, in Paris, little had changed. Of the three French dailies I have worked for as a freelance correspondent in London, all have their offices in central Paris. In the last ten years, centre-left *Le Monde* has moved three times: from the 15th arrondissement to the 5th and then to the 13th. Was the editor-in-chief looking for the best café in town? It's as if the *Guardian* offices had moved from South Kensington to Marylebone and then to Camden. Left-leaning *Libération* has been operating from the 3rd arrondissement of Paris for over twenty years – ensconced between place de la République and gay Le Marais – in a former car park, giving it a certain Guggenheim allure. As for right-wing *Le Figaro*, I have known it always in rue Montmartre in the 2nd arrondissement, near the stock exchange.

No Fleet Street as such in Paris, no Canary Wharf, actually no big, powerful French press conglomerates, which would make a move to the outskirts of Paris worth its while. In Paris, Fleet Street can only be compared to the rue du Faubourg Saint Antoine, which was dedicated to the furniture trade from the French Revolution until about 2000, when it simply disappeared, superseded by franchises of all types such as Starbucks and Foot Locker. Am I saying that in France the press is just like a piece of furniture, a passive thing you sit on or pay a handsome price for to look pretty in your living room? Not exactly, but . . .

11 May 1981, 7.55 p.m. The face of the future French president will soon appear on French TV. I'm nine, my parents are waiting eagerly to know who has won the general election out of Mitterrand and Giscard d'Estaing. My mother tells me to look carefully at the faces of the journalists chatting away before the 8 p.m. results. I remember thinking they looked uptight; their professional smiles looked somehow strained. Now I know why. They knew Mitterrand had won the election and that therefore they had just lost their jobs. Little has changed since. Sure, this is not Italy – how we like to reassure ourselves in France that we haven't yet hit the bottom in terms of freedom of the press – but, in France, the president and his government still appoint public-service broadcasters and have a say, albeit unofficially, in the appointment of presenters and key journalists. How would you like the Queen and the Blair government to appoint *Newsnight*'s editors and presenters? You wouldn't. And neither would I.

On 14 July, Bastille Day, the president traditionally gives a televised interview from the garden of the Elysée Palace. He chooses the journalist who is going to ask the questions his staff has already prepared for him. If the chosen journalist dares to venture outside the carefully scripted guidelines, they will be rapped over the knuckles. You don't mess with the president. Generally speaking, you'll never see a French journalist ask a politician the same question twelve times in order to get an answer, as did Jeremy Paxman with Michael Howard on *Newsnight*, on 13 May 1997. This would be seen as gross insolence in France. In Britain, it's called journalism.

In Britain, hunting down unfaithful husbands, uncovering sex scandals and 'illegitimate' affairs, paying for interviews and signing fat cheques for juicy revelations are also called journalism. One could argue that a country cannot have the best of journalism without its worst, and that if hacks are trained like sniffer dogs, they'll sniff out anything juicy indiscriminately. In France, we've unconsciously chosen the middle road, with small highs and rare lows. French journalists won't grill politicians and rarely invade people's privacy. Respect for private lives seems to go hand in hand with a questionable sense of deference towards the authorities. What can we do, alas?

Paul Webster, famous *Guardian* correspondent who worked in Paris from 1974 to 2004, didn't mince his words about French journalism:

> 'A lot of journalists here hide behind the respect of privacy in order not to do their job and reveal what I think is truly of public interest. When I went to the Nièvre region to research a book about Mitterrand, I found everything there. Everybody knew for instance about his extreme-right connections during and after the war; the local archives revealed it all. Why didn't the French dailies do their job? Only *Le Canard Enchaîné* [3] and the Communist Party daily *L'Humanité* did it, and none of their revelations were taken up.' [4]

France may soon resemble Britain, though. Magazines feeding on banal celebrity gossip have been flourishing in France. The first one, *Voici*, introduced by German media tycoon Axel Ganz in 1981, took some time to take off but has led the way to what we call in French *la presse people*. Now, spin-offs of British titles such as *Clo-Zeur*, oh, sorry, *Closer*, are developing a huge readership in France. The magazine, which carries features such as which stars like oral sex, sold 400,000 copies between July and December 2005. France has caught the celebrity bug, but its investigative journalism hasn't got better. Britain could at least have given France the best as well as the worst of its press, treacherous friend! At the same time, a new breed of French politicians has started playing with fire.

Nicolas Sarkozy, supposedly the most popular politician in

3. The equivalent of *Private Eye*.
4. In an interview he gave to *Libération* on 28 January 2003.

France, has used his wife – as much as she has used him – and his family to act out a family fairy tale. His wife, Cecilia, became his secretary, PR and coach. There was, however, a bumpy six-month period in 2005 when she left him for another with whom she was seen gallivanting around New York. But their reconciliation, a year before the presidential election, took place very publicly in a restaurant where *le tout Paris* have lunch. A few weeks earlier, Nicolas, who is home secretary, by the way, had summoned a Parisian publisher to his office. The latter was about to publish a book about Cecilia, to which she had given the green light. But Nicolas didn't like the look of it. A few hours later, the publisher announced that the 30,000 copies would go in the bin and publication was cancelled. Easy, *la vie*!

In Britain, it's simple too. Once you're in the public eye, you're accountable for everything you do or don't do: the schools you choose for your children, your love life, your tastes, your body, where you go on holiday, what car you drive, etc. Lloyd George could never have been prime minister today. His insatiable womanising would be deemed unacceptable. Needless to say that today his *ménage à trois* with wife and mistress, plus his mistress's two abortions, would cost him the votes of all upstanding members of society – always more numerous than one suspects – and the country's confidence.

When, in France, politicians become accountable for their private lives, something of French civilisation will die. A serial lover with a messy private life can also be a brilliant and dedicated top civil servant, don't you think? Well, OK.

In France, the tyranny of *culture générale* means that a journalist is usually very well educated, sometimes having completed a PhD. So, a French journalist is more an editorialist, a commentator rather than an investigator, who may know little about in-the-field reporting. British journalists by contrast are sleuths. They never take themselves too seriously; there is a job to be done, and it will be done, thoroughly. In France, hacks think they are all intellectuals; they all have an opinion on something. The reporting is often biased from the beginning, as we know what we want to say on any given subject before even researching the facts. Mind you, some of us have interesting things to say, but it sometimes feels as if real research and investigation in the field are left to academics and anthropologists. An upside-down world.

The economics are also radically different in Britain and France. In Britain, the 13 national broadsheets and tabloids have a combined daily readership of about 12 million. In France, the 10 national daily newspapers (including the Communist Party daily *L'Humanité*) have a combined readership of 2 million a day. The huge difference lies in the fact that, in France, there are no tabloids as such and the 'thriving' sector of the press is the weeklies with about 2.2 million sold by just five main titles: *Télérama*, *Le Nouvel Observateur*, *Le Point*, *L'Express* and *Capital*. If the *New Statesman* sold 700,000 copies a week like *Télérama*, you would know more about it.[5]

While in France the dailies' readership is in free fall, Britain's serious daily press is growing, from 2 million in 1965 to 3 million today. A unique situation that defies all odds.

As for the way the industry is run, well, again, we're on two different planets. The end of France's archaic union rules and the inflexible mechanisms of production, distribution and editorial would lead to a healthier press. To quote Simon Jenkins's words when he talked about the American press, I would say that France's 'serious newspapers are declining because they are dull, unworthy and uncompetitive'.[6] If free competition was introduced, so that papers could cut prices and experiment editorially, a lot of French newspapers, perhaps even historical ones, would die, but others, better ones, would emerge.

5. Its current circulation is around 23,000 copies a week.
6. The *Guardian*, 6 January 2006.

Not everything's rosy in the British press, though; it is a harsh and violent world, and, in order to get to the best, you have to wade through piles of rubbish. Still, it is better vibrant than blasé and self-indulgent.

13

London . . .

'In the making of the modern world, Paris and London are related almost as head and body.' Jonathan Jones

I was born and bred in Paris. The genuine article. There is hardly a Parisian paving stone I haven't stepped on, a street corner on which I haven't waited for a friend or kissed a lover, a bridge I haven't crossed, a church in whose wooden saints I haven't confided secrets, a *zinc* upon which I haven't rested my elbows, a *bouche de Métro*[1] I haven't disappeared into or a great restaurant to which I haven't dreamed of taking my dear *papa*, one day, perhaps.

In 1995, I didn't decide to leave Paris; I chose to go to London. I would never desert Paris or France, no need to: they follow me wherever I go. However, in 1995, Chirac was elected president and I didn't fancy living under *Chiraquie*.[2] I'm a patriot, not a masochist.

Why London? Because it was close, an exotic other world for the price of a three-hour train journey. What a bargain. Why London? Because of photographic images in my mind's eye like St Paul's Cathedral standing defiant under a deluge of bombs in 1940; because of literature, the good and the popular, from the Bard to Agatha; because of black-and-white films shot in Ealing; because of British actors James Mason, George Sanders, Rex Harrison, Jeremy Brett, David Suchet, Paul Scofield, Alan Bates, Albert Finney, Richard Harris, Peter Finch and Trevor Howard;

1. Literally a 'Métro's mouth', i.e. a tube station's entrance.
2. In Chiracland.

because of my beloved Great-aunt Marie, married to Tonton Keith, an Englishman I never met; because London was the capital of a country in which Voltaire had seen what was lacking in France. Because of all this and much more.

I chose London, England, Great Britain. I was going to become a Londoner and an Englishwoman. Sounds silly? If you choose to live in a new country, there is no beating about the bush; you really must embrace the culture, eat it, breathe it, learn it, speak it, listen to it. Dive in deep; just try not to drown. I quickly discovered that my surname was difficult to pronounce for an English-speaker. I thought about changing it to my mother's maiden name, Parrot. Doesn't mean anything in French . . . But then I realised Agnes Parrot sounded simply ludicrous, judging by the faces of my new British friends whenever I aired the idea; unless I wanted to embark on a career as a stand-up comedian, that is. As for my first name, I didn't mind being called Agnes; I would introduce myself as such, much easier for all English-speakers. Yet again, Agnes in English is not an easy name to carry off, the image of a great-aunt springs to mind. Only the Irish seemed to like it: Agnes, Lamb of God. All my British friends preferred the sound of my first name in French, so I gave in, and remained French at least in name. I remember one of the first film reviews I did for the BBC. On the presenter's script was written, 'Agnès [An-Yes]'.

Still, I was now a Londoner and I would soon be English. I stopped speaking French, steered clear of anything remotely French-looking or -tasting and fled as soon as I heard my language spoken. I immersed myself in London and a circle of British friends I soon met through a wonderful young English-woman who had become my friend in Paris when we both studied politics. She opened the door to a whole new culture for me and explained the many nooks and crannies most foreigners would take years to discover.

First things first: find a place to rent. What! I cannot rent a flat just for myself? You must be kidding. £430 a month for a room in a flat shared with three other students! As a French person, I wasn't used to the idea of sharing with friends, let alone complete strangers; as for the reality of it, I was totally bewildered. Flat-sharing was unheard of in France in 1995. Could this be why the French can sometimes appear moody, unsociable and arrogant? I decided to abide by local customs. I shared flats in Bayswater, West Hampstead, Kilburn, Camden, London Bridge and a few other places. Ten addresses in ten years. Why so many? Well, I also wasn't used to the daunting figure of the omnipotent landlord, raising hell every six months with 30% rent increases and claiming the flat back for the summer holidays. In France, tenants do as they please, signing six- or nine-year leases with index-linked rent increases.

Becoming a house-owner, you know, *le propriétaire*, wasn't one of my aspirations, so I became a drifting French citizen, sharing flats and getting mad whenever I found the sink piled up with dirty dishes. I would go ballistic whenever my best mate had put the heating on the timer. 'In France, we heat round the clock at a low but comfortable temperature. You backward lot with timers! How can you stand only a few hours of heat a day!' I kept shouting at him. He probably still doesn't know what I was on about. So I wrapped up in layers and layers of woollies and kept the kettle on non-stop from 8 a.m. to 11 p.m. I drank scalding tea by the gallon while my flatmates had their first G&T at 4 p.m. – maybe that was the trick.

Flat sorted, I could now wander around London. *Londres, me voilà!* I walked and walked and walked. Soon, I realised the relative meaning of distances. Paris is a village ensconced inside fortifications. Even if those walls are invisible today, they still map out the Parisians' mental picture of their city[3]. You always

3. Anyhow, *le périphérique*, a ring road, encircles *la capitale* exactly where the ancient walls used to stand.

know where you are; you are either inside Paris or outside. No such thing in London; you're still in London thirty miles from Trafalgar Square.

If you choose to walk in London as I always have – walking being the best way to discover a city and also a Parisian habit – you easily end up walking for four hours a day. It soon becomes a statement rather than an *art de vivre* – deliberate rather than automatic. The same applies to cycling. In London, you must get equipped, insured, carry phosphorescent and flashing lights, get the right maps, think ahead and regularly check your stuff. No room for improvisation, nonchalance or spontaneity of any sort. In other words, you must plan your every move and not worry about looking either like a fanatic walker with sensible shoes and matching rucksack or a mad cyclist with plastered-down hair and black nylon tights. My own unwillingness to trade style for practical clothing made me feel different for the first time, as if I had never really seen myself in the mirror before. As a born Parisian, I ended up combining walking, cycling, public transport and black cabs according to my desires, not to the weather or what I was wearing.

The distance I covered on foot wasn't huge but, still, quite considerable: I'd walk from Shepherd's Bush to Bethnal Green and from Bermondsey to Hackney, through parks, along main roads, down mews and alleyways. Some parts of London, like the East End, seemed devoid of tube stations or any proper public transport. I found it so strange coming from a capital city where there is a Métro station on every corner. Away from the high streets, shops were scarce. Where did Londoners buy their bread and newspapers? Where were the fruit, vegetable and cheese markets? Where were the butchers and fishmongers? Not the ones you could smell half a mile away and not the exclusive ones at Selfridges' Food Hall. Was the alternation between deserted residential areas and bustling high streets to do with the all-too-obvious nostalgia for country living, even right in the heart of the city? Personally, I would die if I ever lived anywhere far from the tube, cafés and food shops.

London appeared so incoherent as a whole, made of bits and pieces, no uniformity, no guidelines, no planning, no global overview. Different local authorities grant building permission without any regard for *l'idée générale*. The most stunning and innovative architecture can be sandwiched between the ugliest buildings on the planet. At the time, I couldn't make head nor tail of it. I was irritated, flabbergasted; it drove me nuts. I was muttering under my breath, swearing even, as I walked through London looking at the buildings. Is that what being French is all about?

However uncomprehending I seemed to be of the urban plan of London, I nonetheless applauded such monstrosity and grandeur side by side. I loved, and still love, the sheer audacity of its architects. What a fantastic playground for ideas and bold statements. The place that always reconciled me to the magnificence and power of London was the view from the narrow metallic red footpath from Embankment to the South Bank parallel to the Charing Cross railway tracks. There, I always knew why I had come to London. There, I always got a sense of history. In Tony Blair's Britain, Dickens didn't feel so far away.

There is no need and no point in comparing Paris with London. The first time I dared to, I immediately regretted it. I told my flatmate that Paris was more beautiful. He replied, sharp as a tack, 'Paris is beautiful because it was never bombed. And why was it never bombed? Because you capitulated.' London wears its scars like a Verdun hero, right on its face; Paris was luckier, left only with internal injuries.

These are two powerful cities, and I love them for opposite reasons. The London of 2000 is 1920s Paris: cosmopolitan, full of energy, daring, heroic, untidy, a microcosm of the world. The Paris of 2000 is quieter, slightly older, a little too clean, though deep down, its soul is intact and its heart is still beating. But is it driven by quiet anger or self-indulgence? Difficult to say. However, whatever you say about Paris, *Paris sera toujours Paris*.

I should let an American in Paris say what I feel:

> We all see our Paris as true, because it is. It is not an old or antiquated Paris that we love, but the persistent, modern material Paris, carrying on in a time of post-modern immateriality, when everything seems about to dissolve into pixels. We love Paris not out of 'nostalgia' but because we love the look of light on things, as opposed to the look of light from things, the world reduced to images radiating from screens. Paris was the site of the most beautiful commonplace civilisation there has ever been: cafés, brasseries, parks, lemons on trays, dappled light on bourgeois boulevards, department stores with skylights and windows like doors everywhere you look. If it is not so much wounded – all civilisations are that, since history wounds us all – as chastened, and overloud in its own defence, it nonetheless goes on.[4]

6 July 2005, Trafalgar Square. I stand with thousands of hopefuls, our faces turned towards the giant screen showing the Olympic Committee ceremony in Singapore. In a few minutes, the world will know who out of Paris or London has been awarded the 2012 Olympic Games. I already know who the winner is. I knew right away when, a few days earlier, I had seen the smile on Tony Blair's face. He was furiously lobbying from his suite at the Singaporian international hotel, while Chirac was making crass jokes about Finnish and English cuisine. Blair was displaying his killer smile *des grands jours*, all gleaming white teeth and sparkly eyes. He knew he had shifted the majority of votes away from Paris (the favourite for months and the stronger candidature) to London. The news on that day didn't come as a surprise to me but as a great relief. London, and Stratford in

4. Adam Gopnik, *Paris to the Moon* (Vintage, 2001).

particular, desperately need the Games in order to get the regeneration and infrastructure they deserve, at long last.

The promotional films said it all. The Paris film directed by Luc Besson cost a fortune and featured film stars such as Deneuve and Depardieu sipping champagne. A picture postcard reminding us of how beautiful Paris was. As if we didn't know already. In comparison, the London film appeared admirably simple, full of the everyday lives of ordinary people, witty and well paced, and it cost ten times less than Besson's exercise in self-indulgence. Grandeur without vision is a dead end.

When I arrived in London, as a keen swimmer, I looked straightaway for a swimming pool, Olympic size of course, fifty metres long. There was one in Ealing and one undergoing work in Swiss Cottage, and . . . and, blimey, that was about it. Others meant hours on a tube and train just to get there. I settled for thirty-metre pools. Even those were difficult to find and were often dirty with open-plan changing rooms. I was always the only one to keep my swimsuit on in the showers, while all the other women stripped off without a second thought. Must be vestiges of the Viking mentality, I thought. What's more, I wasn't allowed to use flippers – 'Too dangerous,' I was told. 'We don't want to be liable.' Come on. Living is dangerous.

In Paris, you can wear swimming accessories like flippers, diver's goggles and gigantic monofins, and swimming pools and public sports facilities can be found everywhere, not always brand new but at least clean. Really glad London won the 2012 bid: I may eventually get a decent pool on my block.

Paris, the capital of romance. I first became aware of this cliché in England when, each time I was asked where I was from, almost on cue, the answer came with a sigh and fluttering eyelashes, 'Ah, Paris, the most romantic city in the world.' I hadn't really thought of it before. What could make it so romantic in the eyes of a foreigner?

Adam Gopnik has the right answer:

This is why Paris is 'romantic': it marries both the voluptuous and the restricted. It is not the yeses but the noes of Paris, not the licences it offers love but the prohibitions it puts in its way that make it powerful. All the noes of French life [. . .] contribute in some odd way to the romance of Paris. Strictness, rules, discipline and boundaries dam the libido, as Freud knew, and make it overflow backward.[5]

London is not romantic, no, London has the violence of a bolt of lightning. London is a city where only the fittest survive, the pulse rises fast and plummets as quickly, things get done and undone in a split second. London is a harsh place for many, where the idle rich can ignore the value of money, but where great ideas are born every day. London is a capital that dares.

5. *Ibid.*

14

Parlez-vous . . . ?

'One parent verbally assaulted me for giving her son detention work in French,' says the Head, who did not wish to be named. 'She asked me why I was giving him such a pointless task.'[1]

English is an extraordinary language. So subtle, so rich, so playful, so flexible, so powerful; it startles the weak, empowers the shrewd and delivers the blows right on cue. Most importantly, perhaps, what is truly admirable is its capacity to absorb foreign vocabulary and make it its own, just like fly-paper.

When I first arrived in London, in 1995, I couldn't believe my eyes or ears: so many French words in the English language, used in broadsheets and tabloids, on radio and TV and, the ultimate test, in the streets. It felt as if there were French words on everybody's lips, as if the British used it as a way of spicing up their conversation.[2] When I say the British, I mean the people I met: cabbies and their '*Voilà!*', plumbers and their 'Your kitchen tap is fucked. Total *merde*, innit?', estate agents and their 'parquet', university friends and their 'I think he has a certain penchant for you, dear', not to mention my PhD supervisor and

1. Guy Woodward, the *Guardian*, 5 November 2002.
2. Linguist Henriette Walter says that 25% of French and English words are related and that both languages have 3,000 words in common.

his '*Ma raison d'être, c'est l'histoire.*' I had just come from a country whose minister for culture had passed a law banning English words from the French language.[3] Journalists, civil servants and theoretically the man in the street had to abide by it. No messing about with the French language! New French words were conceived by an official commission to stop people from using English words. 'Marketing' became *mercatique*, 'email' became *courriel*, etc. And here I was in the UK, a country whose language seemed fearless, fearless of other cultures' intrusions. I was impressed. Just think of it: I learned my Yiddish and my German from the English language.

The odd thing is that French words in the English language are often misused, or even plain wrong. Did you know, for example, that 'double entendre' doesn't mean anything in French? You may wink at your French guest and whisper in her ear, 'Double entendre, darling.' No doubt she'll remain cold. As for 'risqué' it only means 'dangerous' in French and has no double entendre or any *osé* connotation. But this misuse doesn't matter; there is always something titillating about seeing foreigners playing with your (mother) tongue.

The English language is an ogre, and, like all ogres, its digestive capacity is huge. Let us not be naïve; English has become an imperial language. Its vast-reaching empire has implacably imposed its rules on the world, exactly as Rome did in ancient times. English is the new Latin. Linguist Henriette Walter explains that, with time, when all languages have merged into English and been digested, they will then be regurgitated and broken down into different variations of English along geographical lines.[4] This process is exactly how Italian, Spanish, French – and most of English – emerged from Latin.

3. The National Assembly passed Jacques Toubon's law in defence of the French language on 4 August 1994.
4. Henriette Walter, *Honi soit qui mal y pense* (Robert Laffont, 2001).

This idea, that one day the French language will be reborn out of a malodorous English stew, is unbearable to the French, even if it is to take place in a few centuries. For most French, the imperialism of the English language must be fought and will be fought to the bitter end. One must put oneself in their shoes. They like to think that French is the language of freedom and enlightenment, a language that not only coexisted with but, more importantly, nurtured two centuries of political and social progress in the world.

> Why has our language been adopted by the whole of Europe? Is it because of Louis XIV's conquests? Surely not, as vanquished people do not like to speak the victor's language. No, sirs, it is the pleasure of reading French, of feeling and thinking like us that won them over. It is the genius, the order, the sublime, the grace, the light found in our books and within our writers which have made the French language triumphant.

Nothing much has changed in the French psyche since Marivaux pronounced these words in front of the Académie Française – in 1742 – except reality.[5]

The Académie Française was founded by Richelieu in 1635 to stem the flood of Italian and all foreign words in general into the French language as they might prove to be corrupting forces. *Grammairiens*, or grammar experts, were summoned by the kings of France to establish strict guidelines for the use of the language, making it today one of the most corseted languages in the world, which is, of course, not without a certain *allure*.

In any case, after linguists had decided what could be said and

5. The Académie Française is the temple of the French language, where all matters of linguistics are discussed.

what couldn't, the State took hold of the French language. France must be one of the very few countries in the world, if not the only one, where the prime minister is officially in charge of national language policy. The prime minister's cabinet has direct authority over Le Conseil Supérieur de la Langue Française. In France, one can use only words that are correct, authorised by law and sanctioned by the dictionary. However, there have been times of great linguistic invention. During the sixteenth century, Ronsard, Rabelais and Montaigne created many words from Italian idioms. Then again, in the eighteenth century and especially during the French Revolution, *encyclopédistes* printed dozens of new dictionaries filled with hundreds of new words – new words to describe a new world. Presently, however, the French language seems a little slow in catching up with today's constant evolution, especially where new technology is concerned. In France, commissions of *terminologie* create new words, but often too late, as the man in the street has already adopted English words to describe new trends. The English language seems indeed quicker at translating the spirit of the times into words.

However, French resistance has risen to fight off the invader, namely the Anglo-Saxon dialect, once known as English and soon to be the 'language of the world'. Using the latest technology, the freedom fighters of the French language conspire on the web using such sites as languefrancaise.net, langue-fr.net or langue-francaise.org. Every year, langue-francaise.org gives prizes such as La Carpette Anglaise, which we could loosely translate as 'the English Boot-Licker Prize'. It is, they say, 'a prize of civic indignity awarded annually to a member of the French élite who particularly distinguishes themselves in their efforts to promote the domination of the Anglo-American language in France and within European institutions to the detriment of the French language'. It goes on: 'This prize is specially given to the deserters of the French language who, besides being linguistic traitors, behave like slaves to the global financial powers and are responsible for the disappearance of national identities, democracy and humanist social systems.' I can hear you laugh. I would laugh with you, except, deep down, I cannot but admire their rebellious spirit. A desperate attempt at preserving authenticity. Desperate, because it is a fight against an evolution that seems inexorable. Yet the noble defenders of *la langue française* keep fighting, for they strongly believe that a language is not merely a tool of communication, but goes hand in hand with a particular view of the world, a set of values and traditions. For them, the English language is a devastating force of innate oversimplification; it is the language of most Hollywood films, of a people fed on junk food, slaves to a fundamentally unjust economic and social model. Of course, they are wrong. Mind you . . .

Only in France do university professors give papers on 'Is the supremacy of the English language inevitable?'[6] International institutions should, they say, organise a concerted strategy of defence.

> More and more people are being encouraged to use the English language rather than their own mother tongue. As the world is becoming more and more standardised, people are drawn to using a common language. It is progress to see that a growing number of people can communicate directly with each other. Indeed, the Anglicisation of the world doesn't aim at killing indigenous languages but simply at providing a tool for greater comprehension and exchange. However, this perspective is only part of the picture. One cannot deny the profound ties between individual emancipation and political power, between linguistic, social and economical mechanisms, which underlie

6. Roland J.-L. Breto, geolinguist, professor emeritus at the University of Paris VIII.

all relationships between individuals and groups, between culture and collective structure. The rise of an individual within a group depends on his ability to speak the most useful languages. As time goes by, the most valuable language eliminates all others. Cultural imperialism is much more subtle than economic imperialism.

Gosh, we were talking about languages and now it sounds like we are at war.

Let's relax a little and surf on the web to langue-fr.net, whose members like discussing the many aspects of contemporary French and English in a light-hearted way. One quotes a passage from Henriette Walter's book *L'Aventure des mots français venus d'ailleurs* about outdated Anglicisms in the French language. 'All Anglicisms are not necessarily a sign of modernity. The French keep using the words "look" and "coach", but nobody ever speaks any more of "party", "snack-bar", "drink" or "teen-agers". New linguistic fashions have swept away words which we got tired of, proving we didn't actually need them.' A Francophile English-speaker, Joye Lore-Lawson, replies:

I sense that a response is *de rigueur* and *apropos*, and that the members of langue-fr.net, *en masse*, will accord me, its *enfant terrible*, *carte blanche* to comment upon this *fait accompli*. I hope that my *joie de vivre* will provide me a *raison d'être*, and that a *tour de force* of *savoir faire* will spare me any grave *faux pas*. There is a certain *je ne sais quoi* in Walter's passage, but *c'est la vie*, and just a *soupçon* of a *coup d'état* will provide *détente vis-à-vis* the *bête noire* of many *éminences grises*, one that can ruin an *esprit de corps* even among the *crème de la crème*. Such a *cause célèbre* can cause a sense of *déjà vu*, and all that is left is to deliver a *coup de grâce* to those ringing *anglicismes*.

At last, a truce!

Let us forget about imperialism and linguistic war for a minute and just concentrate on the essential: curiosity. Let us leave the semantics and go back to school. Here lies the real danger: 'Only a quarter of state schools are making modern foreign languages compulsory at GCSE. The schools that do offer languages after the age of fourteen are mainly grammar schools and specialist language colleges in more affluent areas.'[7] Two weeks earlier, the Press Association had reported the words of the chief inspector of schools, David Bell: 'French and German may become the preserve of middle-class girls because boys are not interested in learning languages.' The same week, John Dunford, the secretary of the Secondary Heads' Association, declared, 'The numbers are in free fall and we're going to lose a generation of linguists.' How can Tony Blair claim he wants to see more Britons learn a foreign language when he's made language study optional from the age of fourteen? Soon, universities will have to close their modern-language departments one after the other and the Foreign Office will find itself short of competent staff.

When I find myself in a meeting of, say, international film critics or foreign correspondents, there is often one person who cannot speak or understand any foreign language and he (rather than she) is invariably American or British. Everybody else can usually follow a conversation in two other languages. It is, needless to say, slightly infuriating that everybody has to switch to English to accommodate the linguistic deserter.

Another worrying trend: a mere 3% of books sold today in the UK are translations . . . compared with 25% in France. 'If such laxity had applied fifty or sixty years ago, that would have meant, for the English reader, no Kafka, no Camus, no Calvino,

7. Rebecca Smithers, the *Guardian*, 4 November 2005.

no Borges.'[8] The Australian writer Murray Bail once wrote, 'Not to read in translation is unimaginable, almost unforgivable. A lopsided view of the world.'

Faites un effort!

---

8. Oxford professor John Carey, reported by Charlotte Higgins, the *Guardian*, 28 June 2005.

15

Pets

'A conference for pet-lovers in Glasgow was told of a scheme in which young convicted killers, rapists and thieves were given a badly behaved dog to look after. The creators of Project Pooch claim that, in 100 test cases, all the men and pets stayed out of trouble.' Mark Lawson[1]

Here is both a source of hysterical laughter and great wrath. Let's start with the funny side of the British love for pets. Each time I read something like 'Dogs are being stolen at knifepoint in city parks',[2] 'A man appeared at Maidstone Magistrates' Court in Kent accused of the theft of a Jack Russell',[3] 'I have always been crazy for chickens. Chickens will change your world',[4] 'Our four-legged friends can spark a romance – but they can also drive couples apart',[5] I cannot but wonder at the endless-and-quite-honestly-totally-incomprehensible love story between a large proportion of the British people and animals.

1. The *Guardian*, 9 October 2004.
2. The *Observer*, 29 January 2006.
3. *Ibid.*
4. 'Poultry-lover Matthew Rice reveals all', the *Guardian*, 8 October 2005.
5. Justine Hankins, 'The Problem of Having Two Loves in Your Life', the *Guardian*, 15 February 2003.

Mind you, I have nothing against animals; quite the contrary. As a child, I begged my parents over and over again, 'Please can we get a dog?' I wanted a dog, not a cat. I wasn't so much into cats as a stray had attacked me when I was four; it aimed at my eyes and I was almost blinded. But I did like good old big doggies, and still do. I mean dog-like dogs, not sausages on wheels. As a result of my intense lobbying, I got a goldfish. I remember going with my dad not to the pet shop, as there were very few of them in France, but to our local fishmonger's. We had brought a big blue plastic bucket. The fishmonger cupped the fish out of his huge water tank and threw it into our bucket. He informed me solemnly, 'He is the sole survivor of his family: they all got killed by a nasty giant fish. He is seventeen.' The goldfish did look ancient. I named him Daniel. Kids are strange. I didn't even like that name. I had him for five years and then he died on me. It was awful. My mum dealt with it commendably, putting him in a matchbox, which she had padded with cotton wool, and then off he went to goldfish heaven. I remember he was a big eater. Just like me.

That's about it. Did I love him? Yes, I suppose I did, in the same way I loved the pattern on my wallpaper. I didn't think he had a soul, but I did wonder, though, like most kids. I wouldn't have wanted him to be hurt, but I wouldn't have demonstrated for his rights or attacked scientists who might have wanted to do tests on him to find a cure for a deadly disease. Having Daniel in my life didn't make me a better person, and didn't make me into a vegan or even a vegetarian, come to that.

In my book – apart from goldfish because they are too small – fish are meant to be eaten, as are almost all animals on the planet. I don't think we should be cruel to them, of course not, but if hungry, we should eat them. So, producing veal, beef, lamb, pork, ducks, geese, chicken, frogs and snails for our daily consumption is no crime. Humans are omnivorous; we are meant to eat everything, so why should we deny our nature?

In the company of fanatical British animal-lovers, my favourite line is 'But, surely, all animals are made to be eaten, *non*?' I always enjoy the look of sheer horror on their faces. I did it live on a BBC current affairs programme: half of my colleagues laughed; they knew I was being overtly French and provocative; the other half looked at me, utterly disgusted. 'But animals have rights!' gasped one. Rights? I know of human rights, not of animal rights or vegetable rights. It goes without saying that we shouldn't be unnecessarily cruel, but we are not going to hold a special Security Council at the UN just to make a bunch of lunatics happy.

The British are supposed to be animal-lovers and the French, animal-eaters, gobbling down frogs' legs and snails for breakfast, lunch and dinner. Needless to say, this is a slight exaggeration of the truth. I had my first snails when I was about ten. I remember it very well. I was curious to taste them, though it did seem a bit repulsive at the time. I braced myself and bit into the invertebrate. I liked the sauce best: butter, parsley and garlic. My first *rognons*, or ram's testicles: I didn't fancy the idea much, but, damn it, I was in Lyons, and when in Lyons one must go through the offal rite of passage; it's unavoidable. The taste was strong, not one I'd recommend every day. As for my first frogs' legs, it was a few months ago in Normandy after having broken down in the middle of the countryside, late on 14 July. I was simply grateful to have found a very nice *garagiste* against all odds and decided I would celebrate with my first fried frogs' legs and a good Saumur Champigny. I mean, wouldn't anyone? You know what, it tastes just like chicken and there is so little flesh on each leg it's a real rip-off. Again, the best thing was the garlic sauce. I should add that in Phnom-Penh, I had monkey-penis stew. I was only told after the meal. It wouldn't have necessarily been my first choice on the menu, but, well, 'when in Rome . . .' as they say.

All right, so what am I trying to say? Essentially, the Brits love animals to the point of turning into vegan terrorists, whereas the French love animals so much they simply . . . eat them. Same feeling, different application.

Let's have a look at the silly side of British pet passion: better be a whale than an asylum seeker in the UK. There are thousands of associations and charity organisations to help you pamper your pet. Have a look on the Internet, it is just insane. There are doga lessons – yoga for dogs and cats and their owners, so that they can 'breathe and relax in harmony'.

Did you know of the Feline Evolution CatSeat? It's a seat you place on your toilet so that you and your cat can both defecate, not simultaneously, but in the same place. They don't quite explain the purpose of this joint-defecation programme, but no doubt it is to enhance the special bond between you and your best friend.

When I heard about the Missing Pet Bureau offering satellite-operated tags for pets of worried owners, I curled up with laughter. In France, we have a lost-property service, and that's it. In May 2004, the BBC programme *Test Your Pet*, presented by Rolf Harris, was most interesting. Place your pet in front of the TV during the programme and see how he or she reacts to a series of intelligence tests. If they respond, monitor their progress over the week. I'm still waiting to hear the results.

Oh, and mineral water for your pets, courtesy of an American firm whose products are distributed by Scot Pet Food. Pet Refresh, it's called. It has been scientifically proven highly efficient against our four-legged friends' foul breath. The mackerel-flavoured one seems very popular with cats, but how the hell can mackerel improve feline halitosis?

Do you remember when one of Princess Anne's dogs savaged to death one of her mother's numerous corgis? The Royal Family hadn't displayed public grief like this since the Blitz.

Now for when pet passion becomes irritating: the fur ban. Aren't there more noble causes for the red-paint throwers to focus on? Killing animals for the fur trade is indeed rather revolting, especially when you need hundreds of them to make a tiny jacket, but wearing your grandma's 1940s leopard-skin coat is hardly a sin. I certainly wouldn't buy new fur, but I do have a little silver-fox cape, which I bought at the flea market for £40; it's old, warm and beautiful. I also have nothing against using the fur of a rabbit I've just eaten. It's called recycling.

And now for when pet passion translates into dangerous behaviour: animal rights activism. Being completely gaga about pets is at best eccentric and at worst daft but doesn't do anybody any harm. Animal rights activism can be evil. To hound scientists doing their jobs is a disgrace and should be severely punished by law, but, here in the UK, it seems one can get away with bullying, intimidation and even with stealing the body of a dead woman to get what you want. And what do they want? They want to liberate animals; liberate animals from being animals? How do you do that? The Animal Liberation Front was set up in 1976. Couldn't they have helped liberate Palestinians first?

On the other side of the Channel, there are a lot of pets, especially dogs, in the streets of Paris and on the French Riviera, and judging by the daily output of dog shit on the pavement, they certainly seem to be well fed. In fact, I'd say that most of these republican pooches are treated like royalty. The French don't eat canines, but if word went around that *caniche au vin* is to die for, they just might. And they will if there is ever another Commune. My great-aunt's grandmother lived through the Paris Commune; she used to tell how *salons de thé* served rat steaks: 'A little hard to masticate, but I liked the crispy bit.'

16

Pragmatism

'If the Lord God came to England and started expounding his beliefs, you know what the British would say? They'd say, "Oh, come off it!"' George Steiner[1]

'Pragmatism is all right in theory, but never works in practice.' Sidney Morgenbesser

To the question 'Are you a neo-Hegelianist, a naturalist *de la première heure* or a logical positivist?' an Englishman is likely to look wide-eyed and think he's having the piss taken out of him. However, if he is asked whether he is a pragmatist, he is likely to say, 'Yes, undoubtedly, what else can you be?' He even discreetly prides himself on being so. Discreetly? Well, yes, as boasting about anything in England is terribly bad taste, that is apart from your drinking prowess. If you do boast about firmly believing in a concept, ending in an '-ism', you'll probably be thought of as a fascist from the BNP or a pompous lunatic. All words in '-ism' are best avoided. For that reason the Englishman wouldn't expound on pragmatism (which is anyway an American invention[2]); he would go about praising common sense, *le petit*

1. Quoted by Jeremy Paxman, *The English* (Penguin, 1998).
2. Pragmatism originates from the United States, where Charles Pierce first theorised it in 1878.

nom of pragmatism. In other words, a practical approach to problems in life.

Common sense, or a no-nonsense attitude to problems, is a defining trait of the British people. It is not so much a philosophy of action as plumbing for beginners. There is a leak in the bathroom, what do I do?

For example, just after the Second World War menial workers were in short supply, so the throngs of immigrants from India, Kashmir and the Caribbean were welcolmed into Britain: suddenly there's a situation. What do we do? Build housing developments, provide education for their children. Fine. But make them British? No, why should we? They can be our neighbours all right as long as they keep quiet. They have odd ways of living, but, hey, it's their *culture*. Here is multi-culturalism, a practical approach to a practical problem. No underlying principle, no *grands mots*. And as for ideals: leave that to those who are all mouth and no trousers – namely the French.

This is where we get into the argument about pragmatism vs. idealism. Or should I say about Britain vs. France? Pragmatism holds that theory should be tested and verified and that the practical is the basic measure of truth and value. Pragmatism objects to the belief that concepts and intellect represent reality and therefore opposes rationalism[3] and idealism. Idealism is the practice of formulating and living according to ideals – values that one actively pursues, so that what should be, will be.

The British often mock France's motto: *Liberté*, *Egalité*, *Fraternité*. They find it pompous and rather vain; an empty shell that hardly reflects the reality of France. The Brits are totally right. They tend to forget one thing, however: these are

3. Let's leave that bit to another chapter: Locke vs. Descartes.

principles and ideals, an absolute truth and thus a goal that one can aim at but never realise.

British commentator Hugo Young once asked very diplomatically whether 'a touch of pragmatism' could 'bring Europe into new focus'. Basically, he suggested that Europe could work much better if it embraced 'the better side of British culture: practical, constructive and down to the hard, realistic earth'.[4] Forget Europe as an idea, a vision or a romantic construction. What we want is for it to work.

Tory leadership challenger Malcolm Rifkind, when outlining his vision for the future of the party in September 2005, used the same analogy. If the Tory Party had failed in the last three general elections and had fallen out of public favour, it was precisely because the party had lost its true spirit and *raison d'être*: 'common sense and pragmatism over ideological fervour'.[5]

In Britain, even royal pomp has to bow down to the almighty *Dieu* pragmatism. During the royal dinner in the bicentenary celebrations of the Battle of Trafalgar on 18 October 2005, 'Dinner guests *sat* through the royal toast.' This, we learn, is no scandal, it is not 'through rudeness but pragmatism, said to date back to one of the Queen's taller naval ancestors walloping his head on a beam and commanding on the spot that everyone should in future remain seated'.[6]

So imagine when one or two serious British idealist dissidents try to be heard. Take Bob Geldof and his Live 8 for instance. Although his operation was a success in many ways and was embraced not only by millions of UK citizens but the whole world, the British media still make him look like a charming

---

4. The *Guardian*, 7 October 2000.
5. In a speech he gave on 29 September 2005 to the Centre for Policy Studies think-tank.
6. The *Guardian*, 19 October 2005.

passionate fool, but one with business acumen and organisational skills. These last two attributes are what gets him heard, not the fact that he is an idealist with good ideas. Geldof knows all too well that he must dress up his ideas in pragmatic clothes if he wants to be heard and taken seriously. Even then, journalists and commentators from across the political spectrum cannot help sneering at him. For instance, the *Guardian* ran an article about Geldof entitled 'Three months ago Bob Geldof declared Live 8 had achieved its aim. But what really happened next?'[7] In it, journalist Oliver Burkeman says, 'Isn't there a risk, for an idealism-fuelled campaigner such as Geldof, catapulted into the company of world leaders, that one might grow starry-eyed by proximity to power?' A wee bit patronising, *non*? He then continues: 'Perhaps a campaign called Make Poverty History and a series of concerts with the professed aim of bringing the largest mandate in history to bear on the planet's most powerful men were always bound to end in a certain amount of disappointment.' How typical of an Englishman to use self-deprecation and irony to cast suspicion on anything resembling abstraction.

When Robin Cook died on 7 August 2005, as a French observer I couldn't but be astonished by the double-edged eulogy that the former foreign minister received. The right-wing media were, of course, the most critical. The *Daily Telegraph* insinuated that his resignation on a matter of principle – in protest against Britain and the United States invading Iraq without the support of the United Nations – had been a rare political misjudgement because it had achieved nothing.[8] Why should, or even could, an action based on a question of principle translate into practical terms? The ultra-conservative newspaper also sneered at this 'idealist' whose 'intellectual gifts were not

7. Oliver Burkeman, the *Guardian*, 12 September 2005.
8. The *Daily Telegraph*, 8 August 2005.

fully matched by diplomatic or administrative accomplishments'. In other words, Cook may have been a brilliant orator but was, frankly, not enough of a doer. Why couldn't it be enough, and considered as a real achievement per se, to be one of the sharpest MPs Britain has had in a century? No, in Britain, better not show you are clever. For 'Cook had a fine mind, and he knew it.' So Cook was pompous because he was erudite? And here comes the *coup de grâce*: 'Cook could be too clever.' Even the description of his physical portrait is a veiled insult. Cook is described as a 'red-haired with a Lenin-like beard'. Do all red-headed bearded men look like Lenin?

One could ignore this if it was just sneering from the right, but when a left-wing newspaper such as the *Guardian* denigrates Cook's intellectualism in his obituary, one cannot but realise how deeply rooted British suspicion toward abstraction is. Cook is described as an 'impressive parliamentarian', a 'great tactician', a 'brilliant speaker' and . . . an 'intellectual' whose 'intention to conduct an ethical foreign policy gave a hostage to media and political fortune'.[9] As if being principled was anathema to politics and realpolitik the only answer to world affairs.

Cook was a know-all, but so what? Elsewhere, and particularly in France, one can never be too clever; *c'est bon pour la France*. But if an intellectual comes to Britain, he or she must learn the hard way. Just like the American George Steiner. 'When interviewed for a university lectureship, George Steiner made the mistake of declaring his belief in the importance of ideas. "I said to shoot someone because of a disagreement with him over Hegel was a dignified thing to do. It implies that these things matter." He didn't get the job.'[10]

What the British rightly fear is the power of ideas. Since it is sometimes just a small step from a good idea to hellish ideology.

9. The *Guardian*, 8 August 2005.
10. Jeremy Paxman, *The English* (Penguin, 1998).

Furthermore, the British have always been extremely distrustful of the concept nurtured in contemporary France that it is acceptable, sometimes even desirable, to die for an idea. And my fellow countrymen would not be wallowing in endless conversations about *la grandeur de la France* today if it hadn't been for the formidable courage and sheer determination of the British between 1940 and 1945.

The British, therefore, concentrate on what works and what doesn't, while their French friends love to discuss what is a good idea and what isn't. Let's just pause and look at the word 'work'. It stems from the Old English 'wyrcan' meaning 'to work', 'to operate', 'to function'. 'Workmanlike', as in 'efficient', 'no nonsense', is recorded in 1739. Today, work has more than twenty different entries in the English dictionary: to bring to pass, to fashion, to create, to prepare for use, to bring into a desired shape, to keep in operation, to solve by reasoning or calculation, to pay for with labour or service, to bring into some position, to contrive, to practise trickery on for some end, to provoke, to excite, to function according to design, to make way slowly, to be in restless motion, to ferment, to move slightly in relation to another part. The equivalent verb in French, *travailler*, has a much more delimited meaning.

Do you remember Saatchi and Saatchi's first political campaign for a British party – the Tories – in 1979? Their slogan 'Labour isn't working' delivered the right blow. And got Thatcher on the job of . . . making Britain 'work' for the next twelve years. Making things work is the ultimate aim of a British pragmatist, the only measure of success, as in 'hard-working families'. This and money – money being a natural and direct consequence of good work.

The only problem with the pragmatic approach is that it cannot make abstractions work. What works doesn't necessarily make people happy. Happiness is not something you can fix as easily as a leak in your bathroom. 'Quality of life' doesn't refer to high standards of living: expensive car, comfortable house and classy restaurants. When a headline in the *Daily Telegraph* says, 'Bank calculates the price of happiness and it's 2.6 m,'[11] even if said with irony, it is nonetheless a revealing insight into the way the English think.

11. The *Daily Telegraph*, 18 October 2005.

17

Sex . . . or Love?

'Umm, look. Sorry, sorry. Er, I just, umm, well, this is a really stupid question, and, umm, but, er, I just wondered, if by any chance, umm, ah, I mean obviously not because I guess I've only slept with nine people, but . . . but I . . . I just wondered . . . er. I really feel, umm . . . In short, to recap in a slightly clearer version, er, in the words of David Cassidy in fact, umm, while he was still with the Partridge Family, er, I think I love you.' Charles (Hugh Grant) to Carrie (Andie McDowell) in *Four Weddings and a Funeral*

'Tu as de beaux yeux, tu sais.'
'Embrassez-moi.' Jean (Jean Gabin) to Nelly (Michèle Morgan) in *Quai des Brumes*

'Paris est si petit pour ceux qui s'aiment d'un si grand amour.'
[Paris is so small for those who love each other so very much.]
Garance (Arletty) to Frédérique Lemaître (Pierre Brasseur) in *Les Enfants du Paradis*

Here comes the dreaded moment when I must write about sex, or love, according to whether you hail from the shores of Britain or France. And since I speak for both countries – and am writing these lines on the Eurostar in the Channel Tunnel – I am beginning to feel slightly schizophrenic. *Sexe*, *amour*, sex, love . . . what a *cauchemar*. All right, let's get it over with.

I know. The French are supposed to be better at it and do it more often than the English. Every six months in the UK an infuriating survey pops up, the conclusions of which are always published by 'serious' British broadsheets. What a surprise: Every time, the French unfailingly come out at the top of the league. One recent Durex survey stated that the French make love an average of 137 times a year, apparently more than anybody else on the planet.[1] When this kind of silly survey hits the headlines, reactions are always quick to follow, especially from the British and the Americans. The website fuckfrance.com, for instance, lambasted Durex for having got it totally wrong: 'The French are lousy lovers.' Fuckfrance.com gives five main reasons for this:

> 1) France is more a sexual desert than a pleasure garden. 2) The notion of French sexuality, an exported image for centuries, never reflected reality. 3) There isn't a more difficult woman to seduce than a Frenchwoman. 4) The Ministry of Health has set up a telephone helpline for sex problems – and it gets several thousand calls a week. 5) The French have a basic, almost unbelievable ignorance about their own bodies.

Let us look a little closer at this insightful critique. Firstly, 'France is more a sexual desert than a pleasure garden.' I get it; it must be a typing error. They meant 'dessert' rather than 'desert'. Yes, indeed, 'France is more a sexual dessert than a pleasure garden.' A dessert is often a delightfully sophisticated concoction made of fruit from the garden of pleasure. This makes complete sense.

Number 2: 'The notion of French sexuality, an exported

---

1. According to an annual survey by condom manufacturer Durex, October 2004.

image for centuries, never reflected reality.' What the hell do they mean? That the notion of the French being *dieux de l'amour* has always been way off the mark? Obviously. Like all clichés, the notion proves to be partially wrong. There aren't 60 million gods and goddesses of love in France and there aren't 60 million frigid people in the UK – so, the key question really is, is the proportion of *dieux de l'amour* higher in France than anywhere else in the world and, if so, why? But, how can you tell that somebody is a sex god without going to bed with them? Since you can't, even for the sake of research, bed a representative sample of a given population (about 2,000 people), what do you do? And even if you did *coucher* with 2,000 or so people with a funny accent, by what criteria would you judge a sex god or goddess. See, however hard you try, you're *foutu.*[2]

Number 3: 'There isn't a more difficult woman to seduce than a Frenchwoman.' Spot on. The answer is yes. Why? To put it bluntly, because a Frenchwoman is used to being courted, and won't jump into bed at the first wink.[3] She will rarely make the first move and will watch as the man struggles along with his charm offensive. She will judge his every move; sometimes with pity, sometimes with affection, occasionally with admiration. She can prove hard to please. The longer the courtship, the better, as she values determination in a lover. It means he or she is *seriously* attracted to her.[4] However, there are exceptions as *la Française* can at any time exercise her very French right to succumb to *le désir*, that urgent call of the flesh. This doesn't mean, however, that she will find herself in bed one morning with somebody whose name she's forgotten: she doesn't binge-drink. Nor does

2. In other words, you're fucked.
3. I talk about the 'Frenchwoman' as if there was only one kind: this is silly, *évidemment*. Really, I am speaking about myself. After all, this does have some legitimacy, as I am a Frenchwoman (and a Parisian to boot!).
4. Seriousness in all things is a quality for the French. Despite what you may think, seriousness is not *boring*; it is existential.

she binge-fuck. She will expect a man to be gallant and to treat her as an equal. No, this is not a contradiction. *Galanterie* is an elegance of the mind; it is not machismo. Of course, there are as many different kinds of French women, and therefore as many different kinds of attitudes to love as there are types of bread in a *boulangerie*. I will just leave the last word on the subject to Gordon Ramsay:

'My first serious girlfriend was French, and very strong-minded. French and English women are so different. Christ. In England, women are house-proud; everything has to be immaculate. In France and Italy, they're clothes-proud. They aren't interested in searching for a flat or getting a mortgage. And French women are very brash. They're on the verge of, not being uncouth exactly, but they're direct. And they're really, really cold. High-maintenance, demanding and dominant. Bloody hard work. Passionate lovers, though. French women are incredibly passionate. My girlfriend was, anyway. Maybe I just hit on a nympho. Not sure. And it wasn't that I couldn't keep up, precisely, it was just that . . . seven nights a week at two o'clock in the morning, bloody hell! It was like going to bed with a Rottweiler strapped to your chest.'[5]

Number 4: 'The Ministry of Health has set up a telephone helpline on sex problems – and it gets several thousand calls a week.' I have just called the French Ministry of Health: there is no specific hotline for people with sex problems. However, there is a general hotline where you can discuss many different issues, including sexuality, and be redirected, according to your specific problem (concerning STDs, contraception, domestic violence, AIDS, etc.) to the relevant department. Now that every week, thousands of French people discuss matters of sex openly and freely over the phone with public-health representatives, sounds

5. In an interview in the *Observer*, 15 January 2006.

like a good thing, don't you think? In the UK, between 1995 and 2004, diagnosed sexually transmitted diseases (such as syphilis, gonorrhoea, chlamydia, herpes and genital warts) increased by 62%[6]. In the UK, the number of teenage pregnancies is three times higher than in France. So either the British are sex maniacs or it's down to a lack of education and openness. This is certainly a different attitude from that in France where sex is talked about in a relaxed, serious and unembarrassed way.

Number 5: 'The French have a basic, almost unbelievable ignorance about their own bodies.' Do they? One thing is sure; in France, the naked body is often seen in an artistic or aesthetic light not simply a machine. Is the way the French look at the body influenced by their Catholic heritage? No doubt. At least as much as Protestant puritanism has shaped the way you look at it. Guilt-ridden pleasure vs. matter-of-fact indifference.

Paradoxically, clichés about the French are often nurtured and passed down through the generations by foreigners. At home, the French don't go on about their, say, supposed sexual prowess. You're never really aware of how you're perceived until you start travelling or living among foreigners.

Have you seen *Gigi*, Vincente Minelli's 1958 musical based on Colette's novel? Hollywood takes a peek at France and what do they see? Love everywhere. Gigi, played by Leslie Caron, is both entranced and outraged:

> *I don't understand the Parisians,*
> *Making love every time they get the chance.*

She goes on:

> *I don't understand the Parisians,*
> *Wasting every lovely night on romance.*
> *Any time and under every tree in town,*
> *They're in session two by two.*

6. According to Avert, the AIDS charity.

> *What a crime with all there is to see in town,*
> *They can't find something else to do.*
> *When it's warm, they take a carriage ride at night,*
> *Close their eyes and hug and kiss.*
> *When it's cold, they simply move inside at night.*
> *There must be more to life than this!*[7]

Little has changed in the world psyche since Gigi pronounced these words.

So goes the adage: the French are obsessed with love. And the British are obsessed with sex. The French take love seriously, while the British can only snigger uneasily as if petrified by the fear of releasing pent-up emotion. The French welcome the complexities of love, while the British would rather concentrate on the mechanics of sex in order to avoid the intricacy of love, etc., etc. We could develop this argument ad nauseam. This contrasting portrait is one of two kinds of people and two kinds of psychological profiles rather than one of two nationalities. My own experience is that people transcend these archetypal behavioural patterns. However, there are certainly penchants, habits and attitudes that are deeply rooted in the national psyche of both countries, and which may explain the enduring clichés.

Eroticism. Tabloid front pages vs. lingerie ads: worlds apart. Take the average UK citizen. As they leave home in the morning to go to school/university/work, they undoubtedly pass a news-stand where oodles of flesh leap out at them. Every day, a whole new range of Barbie dolls vie for page-3 status, striking unfortunate poses, showing their enhanced rears and baring their fake breasts. Their charms are devoured by millions of readers, yet they seem unconcerned. The problem is not the naked flesh; (*au contraire*) it is the casualness with which it's shown. As if flesh were somehow disconnected from the soul. I

7. Lyrics by Alan Jay Lerner and music by Frederick Loewe.

know, this sounds like pompous balderdash, yet this is how a French person thinks. To a French spectator, tabloid-front-page girls certainly look 'fit and healthy', even if artificially enhanced, but they are rarely attractive because the way they are photographed is soulless. The word 'fit' brings us back to how the naked body is considered by both cultures. 'Fit' means in good shape, well conditioned, ready for service, sound, just like a car after passing its MOT. How on earth could this mean 'attractive'? Yet it does in Britain, as 'fit' has become the latest compliment to give a girl. In France, 'fit' means 'fit'; that is to say boring, really.

In France, when the average Parisian walks from home to the Métro on their way to work, they will undoubtedly pass lingerie shops and lingerie ads. What other than the collection of Aubade ads, which have hypnotised France for the past thirteen years, to epitomise *érotisme à la française*? These black-and-white ads stop passers-by in their tracks to stare and marvel in the middle of the street. Next time you're in France, look out for them; men and women, old and young, looking at these ads as if they were paintings in the Louvre. There is usually an appreciative smile on their face and a sense of wonderment too. Some even look lost in contemplation. Needless to say, Aubade ads feature a scantily clad female body. You never get to see the face of the curvaceous model. It's not X or Y celebrity showing off her beautiful body; no, it's an unknown woman; it could be you or me.[8] No need for identification with any particular person. That is not the point. *C'est la femme* that interests us here. Her body is on view in *clair obscur*, so you're never quite sure whether you're admiring the curves of her magnificent *derrière*/bosom/back/ thighs/shoulders/arms or their enhanced shadows on the wall.

8. It can be you if you wear Aubade, the brand implies. It has almost trebled its profits since the campaign started, rising from €15 million to €40 million.

In the corner of the poster, there is an enigmatic and humorous message in the form of 'Lesson number . . .'[9] Imagine beautiful curves veiled in see-through black lace or virginal white satin with these words: *'Leçon numéro un: feindre l'indifférence.'* You can almost hear the husky voice advising, *'Leçon numéro deux: s'il résiste, pratiquez l'hypnose,' 'Leçon numéro six: détourner la conversation,' 'Leçon numéro dix-sept: mettre à l'épreuve son self-control.'*[10] And so forth. These ads have the effect of a beautiful *gâteau* in the window of a *pâtisserie*: whetting your appetite. Not quite the same effect as the piece of dead turkey thrown at you every morning from a London news-stand. One makes you drool; the other gives you nausea.

Seduction. Seduction is a *modus vivendi* in France. One revealing thing is the word's meaning in both languages. In English, 'seduction' has a double-edged meaning; it can be a straightforward enticement but may also imply the use of deception. There is often an element of danger and treachery. In French, *la séduction* is all about attraction and charm with no sense of impending doom – i.e. no need to feel frightened. It is true that games of seduction are not widely practised in the UK; it is certainly not a national institution as in France. What you do, however, is flirt.[11] I have always found flirting *à l'anglaise* a most irritating affair, as no risks are being taken. It's all affectation. An Englishman who flirts is no more than a *poseur*. Seduction *à la française* is about taking risks as it can go very far. If you play, you must be prepared to lose all. This national hobby is played out every day in the streets of France, its offices, supermarkets, schools, universities and its homes. First, the look. People look at each other, discreetly or shamelessly. Complete

9. We have now reached Lesson number forty-three.
10. 'Lesson number one: feign indifference,' 'Lesson number two: if he resists, hypnotise him,' 'Lesson number six: change the subject,' 'Lesson number seventeen: test his self-control.'
11. From the French *compter fleurette*.

strangers compliment each other on how they're dressed or made up. A woman will stop a girl on a bus saying she loves the way she has done her hair. While waiting at the traffic lights, a young man will tell an elderly woman that he finds her very elegant. She will thank him and they will part without another word. Seduction is not always sexual. There is a broader picture to it. Seduction is *un état d'esprit*. It's all about appreciating with the eyes what you cannot always (nor would necessarily want to) taste with the mouth.

Let's move on to the cinema. Have you ever seen a French movie? Most of them convey the typically Gallic seductive spirit. Think of French actresses, from Michèle Morgan, Danielle Darrieux, Jeanne Moreau to Brigitte Bardot, Catherine Deneuve, Carole Bouquet, Juliette Binoche, Sophie Marceau and Audrey Tautou. Very different types of beauty, different characters, yet they appear to you as undeniably French. Why? What do they have in common? Freedom, *mystère*, passion, a slight aloofness, perhaps. They certainly don't reveal all. They've got allure and chic. You never quite understand what they're about; that's the attraction. There was a time when British cinema featured exactly the same kind of women – and men – destined to live love and passion to the full, in the same way the French did. Just remember: *It Always Rains on Sunday*, directed by Robert Hamer, starring the wonderful Googie Withers; *Saturday Night and Sunday Morning*, directed by Karel Reisz, and *This Sporting Life*, directed by Lindsay Anderson, with the magnificent Rachel Roberts; *The Prime of Miss Jean Brodie*, directed by Ronald Neame, starring the stunning Maggie Smith; *The Go-Between*, directed by Joseph Losey, featuring the irresistible Julie Christie; *Agatha*, directed by Michael Apted, with the incredible Vanessa Redgrave. And their leading men certainly matched the intensity of these women's emotions. They were Richard Harris, Albert Finney, Robert Stephens, Alan Bates . . . Today, who are the leading men of British cinema, *les séducteurs anglais*? Hugh

Grant. Er, right, the inadequate forty-something public-school bachelor figure. Thank God for Daniel Craig. If only he looked – how shall we say? – brainier. There is also Chiwetel Ejiofor. If only he chose his films more carefully. There is Ralph Fiennes, another brilliant actor, with brains and sensitivity. If only *le garçon* oozed more sensuality. So what happened between the late 1970s and today? How come French cinema is still focused on love, desire, passion and seduction as much as it was during the 1930s of Jean Vigo and Jean Renoir while British cinema seems to have simply given up? Capitulation is not your style. Maybe American puritanism has polluted your screenwriters' imaginations.

Seduction as a national sport has its disadvantages, as it doesn't leave much room for neutrality. In the workplace, French men's attitudes don't change much from the ones they display in the street: they will compliment you on the colour of your new lipstick or the shape of your skirt and will always see you first as a woman, then as a colleague. You can imagine the frustration. I have a French journalist colleague who always avoids answering awkward questions from a female colleague by telling her, 'You're so beautiful.' What can she do? She is not going to sue, is she? This is not the custom in France. It would be judged as silly and American. So a Frenchwoman is brought up accordingly; she will dodge suitors with a firm smile, not a punch in the face or a lawsuit. However, there are times when a Frenchwoman wishes she were American.

Last but not least, in France, love and sex are important matters. Important, not necessarily as in 'serious' but certainly as in 'significant'. It can be light and playful, but it cannot be casual (casual as in careless). In the UK, there sometimes seems to be a national consensus: best keep sex casual, inconsequential, in other words physiological.

Faites vos jeux, rien ne va plus.

18

Small Talk

'The first duty of a man is to speak; that is his chief business in the world; and talk, which is the harmonious speech of two or more, is by far the most accessible of our pleasures. It costs nothing in money. It is all profit. It completes our education, founds and fosters our friendships, and can be enjoyed at any age and in almost any state of health.' Robert Louis Stevenson[1]

'Talk to yourself in the mirror. Make a random list of topics and see what you have to say on the subjects. Tennis, Russia, butter, hip-hop, shoes – the more varied your list, the better.' Rule six of 'How to Make Small Talk'[2]

I had never heard of the concept of 'small talk' until I arrived in England at the age of twenty-three. At first, I was in awe. Most of my British friends could bond with complete strangers with such ease: I thought it was admirable. They engaged in conversation with them – babies, youngsters and elderly alike – on the most inconsequential subjects: weather, gardening,

1. In his essay *Talk and Talkers* (1882).
2. 'How to Make Small Talk', *How to Do Just About Everything in the Office* (Collins, 2004).

anything really, a few exclamations and interjections, and there they were keeping the little fire of civility burning.

At dinner parties, they oozed confidence and won people over they had never met before by making them laugh at their own expense. I later learned that this particular trait was called self-deprecation, upon which British civilisation was built. This is perhaps Britain's greatest achievement and most valuable contribution to the world's well-being: its ability to laugh at oneself.

The French are not as civil as the British; no such thing as small talk, as, quite honestly, one rarely wants to engage with strangers there. Talk to them? What for? Why would anyone want to engage with, say, a taxi driver in Paris? Most of them are crooks, misogynists and Lepénistes. Beyond the all-too-easy caricature, the French are indeed less inclined to make efforts for the sake of civility. Courtesy, is not a French forte. A British friend who has recently settled in Paris asked me how to say, 'Hope you're well,' 'Sorry for disturbing you,' 'Thank you for your help,' 'I would be most grateful,' etc. when sending emails and making calls to get information. My answer was quick and curt: 'Don't bother: you don't write or say those things in France.' He persisted, being brought up to be polite. After a few weeks, he had stopped trying: telling someone, 'Sorry for disturbing you,' is already wasting their time. One should get to the point, no need to be ultra-polite; it won't get you anywhere. It could even be seen as suspect: 'Why is he being so nice to me? There must be something behind it.' In France, over-politeness is seen as deviant hypocrisy, i.e. obsequiousness.

In England, I discovered the concept of small talk through social interaction. Wherever I went I was greeted by an avalanche of hilariously witty one-liners on all sorts of topics. Personally, I couldn't compete, my English wasn't good enough; besides, one needs to be born into 'small talk' to do it well. I couldn't play the game as well as somebody who had been breast-fed small talk from infancy. So I remained mostly silent and just enjoyed listening to my friends. It somehow reminded me of *conversations spirituelles* one can hear at French dinner parties. That sort of intercourse and small talk are of a different kind but in fact share common roots.

Baldassare Castiglione's *Courtisan*, published in 1528, Erasmus and his much-copied *Civilité puérile*, which came out in 1530, and Giovanni della Casa's *Galateo*, written in 1558, all provided recipes for the man of the world on how to talk and behave with distinction and wit in the company of peers and high-class womenfolk. These 'guides' taught gentlemen to appear measured in all circumstances and to show through conversation that they are of a likeable, adaptable and polite nature. Gentlemanly conversation should avoid being dull, vulgar, pedantic and satirical at all costs.

The eighteenth century went on to make conversation an art, which banished seriousness; puns and wit became a must. In the milieu of French aristocracy, a man of no wit was a dead man and frivolity was pushed to the limit.

To counteract the vanity of such practice, authors such as Stendhal tried to restore depth and *naturel* to *conversations de salon*. With the revolution knocking at the door, conversation inevitably became more substantial. Matters of life and death replaced *calembours*, or puns. This was a significant turning point: frivolity belonged to the Ancien Régime. The revolution transformed conversation once and for all into a passionate philosophical and political debate. Everything became political and all topics soul-searching.

Throughout the nineteenth century and to this day, French conversation has followed both trends. Varying in content according to the *milieu*, conversation usually includes both *bons mots* and intense discussions on existential subjects. Meanwhile, in England, a line was drawn between, on the one hand, erudite conversation and, on the other, the all-inclusive banter providing effortless pleasure. Erudition was left to 'specialists' – i.e. experts and academics – while small talk was left to everybody else. In France, everybody likes to think they are a specialist on all subjects.

I spent my childhood attending lunches and dinners that lingered on throughout the afternoon and into the evening and during which voices were often raised and people would be called names, such as *Staliniste* or, even worse, *Trotskyste*, before the second course had even started. Certain topics, such as the Second World War and Algerian independence to name but two, didn't generate many *bons mots*, just plain *fâcherie*[3] more often than not. That was normal. In France, siblings, best friends and colleagues are supposed to quarrel bitterly and part before dessert is served. Some end up not talking to each other or acknowledging each other for years. *C'est la vie*.

As a teenager, I remember hearing the crystalline laughter of Proustian dinner guests through my bedroom wall, whose wit and *mots d'esprit* were passed from one *convive* to another like salt and pepper. However, this laughter was sometimes followed by deathly silence when those present jousted over international politics. I remember hearing one guest noisily getting up from his chair, slapping his napkin down on the table and storming out. He had just had an argument with a fellow diner on the subject of the aftermath of the 1989 events in China. He objected to France opening her doors to all Tiananmen dissidents. In France, the ebb and flow of genial conversation encompasses the lightest and the heaviest of subject matters. In France, one doesn't grow up thinking there is 'small' and 'big' talk.

Could it indeed be compulsory teaching of philosophy[4] at A level in French *lycées* that explains the French habit of

3. A massive row that leaves people estranged for a long time.
4. A beginner's introduction, really.

embracing abstract topics between two servings of *poulet rôti* and green beans just before the latest joke on Chirac's top ten gaffes? Anthony Burgess wrote that, for the French, 'Philosophy can only come to life in the bedchamber or over *coq au vin* or before the firing squad.' He called it 'the existential marinade'.[5]

Is it their love for *idées générales* that makes them assert truths with total confidence in front of friends and perfect strangers alike, while giving a shrug of the shoulders and following up with the usual, *'C'est une évidence!'* Australian writer Murray Bail has an interesting theory on the peculiarities of European writers, which can be applied to continental conversation:

> Europeans [. . .] are not afraid of the bold assertion. So bold and distinctive are these assertions, it's enough to send timid and ordinary minds rushing for the exits. 'Oh, that's a generalisation.' [. . .] Timid thinkers are more comfortable when bold and distinctive minds are lowered to more digestible levels – via the refuge of relativism [. . .] The bold assertion coming in at an unexpected angle: it forces the interlocutor to sit up, and either agree or not. It can be as jolting as a slap across the face. A speaker sometimes can gain satisfaction only by provoking a duel. By 'generalising', he throws off an infectious energy.[6]

The energy of the conversation often felt during a French dinner party comes from that exuberant mix of nonsensical declamation, outrageously misinformed twaddle and inspired strokes of genius. In *Paris to the Moon*, Adam Gopnik, Paris correspondent for the *New Yorker* from 1995 to 2000, recalls how he finally accepted that every French citizen philosophises like a philosopher and that it should seem absolutely normal:

5. Anthony Burgess, *M/F* (Penguin, 2004).
6. Murray Bail, 'Continental Shift', the *Guardian*, 10 September 2005.

'I love to study the problem of being,' said Robert, one of the oldest *garçons* at the Balzar [. . .] I thought the most irritating thing about life in France, [. . .] the insistence on the primacy of the unspecific, on turning things into abstractions of themselves at every turn, was actually a gift [. . .] France is marked by a struggle between its pompous official culture and its matchless vernacular, commonplace civilisation – and that what makes France unique is that so much of the pompous, abstract, official culture has spilled over into the popular 'culture', so that every man sees himself as an aphorist, his own Montaigne in his own tower.

A typical successful French dinner party consists of, first and foremost, a menu, which titillates the palate and stimulates the mind. Then, a lively political and philosophical debate, peppered with frivolous anecdotes, a sprinkling of absurdly silly statements, a few astoundingly well observed and brilliant remarks, some good puns and two or three good ideas to chew over for the next week or so.

In England, only a fool would bring up *grandes idées* at a dinner party. If you must talk about serious matters, make sure you camouflage your thoughts with humour. Taking yourself seriously meets with universal disapproval, unless you're a foreigner, that is.[7] Acceptable subject matters usually revolve around buying and selling properties, sharing tips on mortgages and the cost of children's education, all of which make the situation slightly awkward for those whose existence has long been dominated by long-term tenancies and incorrigible serial lovers procrastinating over the question of reproduction as long as possible.

In England, conversation has been divided between the acceptable 'small talk', which is pleasant, non-committal and

---

7. In this case, almost anything's acceptable, as you don't belong to the club.

inclusive, and 'big talk', which is serious, boring, pedantic and exclusive. So no 'big' conversations at an English dinner party. As TV presenter, author and scientist Dr Jonathan Miller puts it, 'Conversation is not an art and big conversation bores me.'[8]

The difference in national temperament between the UK and France has certainly not been lost on small-talk experts. In the 'warnings' section of a recent book, *How to Do Just About Everything in the Office*, one reads, 'Keep your fellow chatterers in mind; naughty stories and loose language will be frowned upon in many circles. Similarly, your French quips and scientific discourses will be wasted on some.'[9]

Recently, British academics and commentators have been in despair about the civilised art of small talk being hijacked by banal chit-chat. According to Ronald Carter, conversation expert and professor of English language at Nottingham University, 'Brits have lost the skill of conversation. We have got used to chatter and have stopped making the effort to reach any more significant conversational depth. Too much chatter means we keep our real thoughts to ourselves. We risk becoming rigid and thoughtless in our opinions.'[10]

The same sense of doom has also gripped France, where temples of conversation, such as cafés, have declined in number and even been partly replaced by Starbucks, the first franchise to have invaded that most sacred public place, *le café*. Today, there are fewer than 47,000 cafés in France, for a total of 58 million inhabitants. In 1900, there were 510,000 cafés for a total of 42 million people. With the slow disappearance of *le café* in French daily life, France is witnessing the slow death of public debate and conversation.

8. Reported by Amelia Hill, the *Guardian*, 20 February 2005.
9. 'How to Make Small Talk', *How to Do Just About Everything in the Office* (Collins, 2004).
10. Reported by Amelia Hill, the *Guardian*, 20 February 2005.

In the UK and in France, optimistic observers claim that Internet chatrooms and phone texting have replaced conversation as we knew it in the last century. If this is true and small talk can easily be conveyed by SMS, what about big talk? Could the next French revolution, currently simmering in the French *banlieues*, be one day launched by a single txt-msg? In txtspk, that would be: 'lts torch ze Bstll & all ze mother-fkrs!'

19

The English and French Left

'The fatalism on the French Left is not because of globalisation; it's because of the wretchedness of Mitterrand's bequest and its own inadequacy. The British Left has different options. For a start, it has a legacy of success on which to build and a majority coalition that is still holding together.' Will Hutton[1]

I had been thinking about it for some time. My older brother already belonged to the Montmartre cell. I had toyed with the idea for a year and was waiting for my thirteenth birthday. Then I took a leap and grabbed the phone. A young man, three times my age, answered.

I blurted out, 'I want to join the Socialist Party, monsieur.'

'Aha, where do you go to school?'

'Picpus in the twelfth arrondissement.'

The voice became brusque and slightly suspicious. 'And why, exactly, does a pupil at a Catholic school want to join the Mouvement des Jeunesses Socialistes?'

'Er, because I'm a socialist,' I replied timidly.

'Very well, then. There is no *cellule* in your area; you'll have to go to place d'Italie in the thirteenth. Meetings take place twice weekly in the evenings.'

1. The *Observer*, 7 August 2005.

How on earth was I going to tell my right-wing Gaullist dad that I had to take the tube in the evenings, to go to socialist meetings in the louche 13th arrondissement?

After I had noted the address of my cell, the *chef de section* added one last crucial thing: 'By the way, one never says *vous* in the Socialist Party.' What a killing one-liner. I had said *vous* to the guy simply because I was thirteen, he was much older and because, bloody hell, one says *vous* to people one has never met before. What an idiot, I thought. *Quel con!* If there is one thing I hate it is inverted snobbery. This, I'm afraid, has defined the French Left for the past forty years.

I never joined the French Socialist Party.

If only François Mitterrand had answered the phone, we would have got along fine. In the 1980s, as legend has it, an eager new member of the Parti Socialiste addressed Mitterrand during a party conference, 'Hey, François, now that I have joined, I can say *tu* to you!' '*Si vous voulez,*' replied Mitterrand, as quick as the snake that he was.

Though I was never a party member, I have voted for them at almost every single election since I could first vote in 1990. Like most French youngsters, I also voted Communist – you have to, it's a kind of political rite of passage in France – as well as the Ligue Communiste Révolutionnaire. I have, however, abstained from voting for any Communist or Trotskyite parties since my late twenties, no doubt *le ridicule* would have eventually been too much for me. I may be an intellectual proletarian, but I've never worked in a factory and I certainly don't condone Stalinism or Trotskyism. No, really. At the age of thirty, one develops a certain logic. Even for a French citizen, political romanticism has its limits.

Having said that, I wouldn't mind stirring up a *coup d'état* within the Socialist Party in order to get rid of all the oldies who have killed the French Left and who thus offer voters no alternative to Nicolas Sarkozy, France's interior minister and second-in-command. Sarkozy? You know, France's midget Jack-of-all-trades who takes himself for the French Thatcher.

Many British commentators see France at a turning point; they are right. Except that they think France today finds herself in the same predicament as Britain in the late 1970s, with all-powerful unions and an archaic economy. It is also exactly what Sarkozy and a new breed of French right-wingers would like us to believe. They say, look at the mess France is in; what the country needs is a French Maggie – Sarkozy, and QED.

French and foreign commentators should know better: France is always in a state of crisis, that's her *modus vivendi*. She evolves through hiccups, crises, turmoil, revolts, street fighting. That's the way it is, rightly or wrongly. The French want a strong state, always did.

Sarkozy wants to trigger his own little revolution by denying centuries of history. A great advocate of all things American and British, he'd like to turn the French into ultra-liberals, in the economic and philosophical sense of the term. And why not? Mind-boggling as it sounds, he thinks he can succeed. How come he feels so confident? Because there is nobody to stop him; certainly not the Opposition.

Indeed, what Opposition? The French Left has almost dissolved and its remains stink of self-indulgence. The French champagne socialists obviously eat too well, too much, too often. Today, as a result, the Parti Socialiste is an empty shell, which has failed half of the French people, who are now left out on a limb. Since the end of the Cold War, the party seems to have lost its points of reference, unable to adjust to globalisation in a post-materialist era. No questioning, no distance, no self-criticism and, worst of all, no new ideas. Jean Jaurès, help!

On 21 April 2002, when the Socialist Party's leader and France's prime minister, Lionel Jospin, found himself out of the second round of the general election, losing to fascist Jean-Marie Le Pen, he couldn't think of anything more useful to do than to play the *vierge outragée*. It was suddenly all about him when obviously it was all about France. Jospin theatrically announced his retirement from political life, deserting his compatriots at one of the gravest times in the country's political life. *Merci beaucoup*.

Since 1995 and Chirac's arrival in power, the French Socialist Party has been on a death wish, choosing to rest on its Marxist laurels, banqueting on the Left Bank while waiting cheerfully for France's Armageddon. At the same time, Tony Blair, Gordon Brown and a few others have set their vote-winning machine in motion, bagging three general elections in a row. And how did they do it? A massive clear-out. Everything must go. The British Labour Party had never been Marxist – at least that was one thing Blair and his acolytes didn't have to get rid of. Everything else, they chucked out. They kept the shell, repainted it and changed its name to New Labour. New is good; always is in the marketing world.

However, in order to win elections, they had to appeal to key people. To the City's big shots they said, 'Don't be afraid; we are no reds, we love money.' And to populist Murdoch to get the support of his press, 'Don't worry, Rupert, we won't join the European currency.' And to the voters, 'We'll fight the forces of conservatism, the cynics, the élites, the establishment.' What the people hadn't realised was that Blair et al., his businessmen and demagogic tycoon friends had superseded the old establishment to become the new cynical establishment, all the more dangerous as all its members were tied more than ever before by the bonds of money.

The new élite is held together by a desire for personal enrichment, its acceptance of capitalism and the need for the profit motive, while the resistance to money values is much weaker and former anti-capitalists have been the people least inclined to criticise them once in power. As government depends more on private investment and party donations, both ministers and permanent secretaries come closer to bankers and corporate chiefs: the centre of gravity of the power world is shifting away from Westminster towards the City. The new establishment looks more like one giant boardroom, linked by common interests and agreements. New Labour has proved more sympathetic to big business than any post-war government except Margaret Thatcher's.[2]

So this is where we are at: intellectual mediocrity in Paris and greed in London. *Et le peuple dans tout ça?*

2. Anthony Sampson, *Who Runs This Place?: the Anatomy of Britain in the 21st Century* (John Murray, 2004).

20

The Monarchy

Ah! Ça ira, ça ira, ça ira!
Les aristocrates à la lanterne.
Ah! Ça ira, ça ira, ça ira!
Les aristocrates on les pendra.
Popular French refrain from 1790[1]

France was once a monarchy; so grand, it had to fall. England was once a republic; so brief, no one can remember. Modernity was born in 1789, both for the French who were reborn as a nation from aristocrats' blood and for the British who watched the spectacle with sheer horror or unseemly titillation. Since then, as Jonathan Fenby once wrote, 'The example of France stood in counterpoint to the essence of the English political system.'[2] France and England became flipsides of the same coin, each other's negative.

Since 1789, France has experimented with as many political regimes as she could think of: revolutions (bourgeoise and proletarian), empire, parliamentary monarchy, commune, republic

---

1.   *We will win, we will win, we will win!*
        Take the aristocrats to the lamp-post!
        We will win, we will win, we will win!
        The aristocrats will be hanged!
2. Jonathan Fenby, *On the Brink: the Trouble with France* (Abacus, 2002).

(five different forms), state collaboration with Nazism, resistance. In 200 years, France has seen 11 different political regimes, while all the time the British Royal Family has been perfecting its skills at croquet.

Since 1789, Britain has lived under only one political system: a parliamentary monarchy, which successfully fought attempts to invade her shores, both by Napoleon and Hitler – not that I wish to compare the two. This system obviously suits the British psyche and has been a guarantee of political tranquillity and social stability for centuries. British neighbours have never tried to behead each other (to my knowledge) and no duke's head has ever had the honour of adorning the country's lamp-posts.

Despite such extraordinary achievement and many reasons for pride, the reaction of some of my British friends whenever I speak of Britain as a monarchy has always bewildered me. They would often stubbornly resist, showing anger that seemed rather continental. 'No, Britain is not a monarchy! The Queen is a mere puppet, she has no power!' they'd say, simmering with rage. 'Sorry, but Britain is a monarchy, a parliamentary monarchy and a great democracy; just look it up in the *Oxford English Dictionary*,' I'd reply, slightly *vexée*. 'As for the Queen, she does have powers, actually; she just knows better than to use them, that's all.' The acrimonious conversation would drag on, every argument met with a denial and would finish in deep mutual annoyance. Another contentious Anglo-French topic, I thought, but one with no *raison d'être* whatsoever.

After the same scenario had occurred unexpectedly a dozen times with different people, I wondered what could lie behind such bizarre behaviour, at least seen from a French point of view. I could only construe some psychological conclusions. These liberal friends of mine react so strongly because they must somehow feel ashamed. They have managed to create for themselves an idea of Britain as a true and great democracy with the monarchy as no more than a painted backdrop on a Hollywood set. They have convinced themselves that, really, Britain is not a monarchy. In their book, members of the Royal Family are just another troupe of Morris dancers, providing occasional comic relief and folklore for tourists. In fact, it would be simply unbearable for them to acknowledge that they actually live in a political system in which they are not citizens but subjects. If they did, they would have no choice but to either leave the country in order to live up to their principles or actively campaign for a change of regime. So they have created this fantasy world where Buckingham Palace stands for Britain's own Disneyland, a valuable national enterprise, which attracts tourists and fills the nation's coffers with foreign currency. The fact that this Disneyland actually owns huge chunks of the country hasn't quite entered their minds and their carefully constructed vision of Britain.

Stephen Frears, the first film director to make a film about the living members of the Royal Family, *The Queen*, argues that:

'It is not very healthy really to live in a Monarchy such as ours. We live a permanent contradiction and a permanent lie. We think we are citizens when actually we are subjects. It keeps us in a kind of infantile state. Do you realise that the Queen is the only person to have stayed in my life for so long? I have always known her, she's been with me longer than my mother or my wife.'

When I was born, de Gaulle was already dead. How many presidents have I known? Only four, Mitterrand and Chirac being elected twice each, and fourteen prime ministers. But the Queen is here to stay. After her, there'll be her eldest son (ouch!) and then his eldest son and so forth. A little monotonous, perhaps?

In France, the people like to decide for themselves, not that they necessarily know better, but, hey, once a *sans-culotte*, always a *sans-culotte*. I wonder where the French people are going to lead France next: another revolution? Quite possibly. A new political regime and the Sixth Republic? Hopefully. Difficult to say, really, as they are a very unruly people. They always seem to need a strong man and a strong state to control them, but not a king and a monarchy. They've been there, done that.

Originally, I thought that maybe, one day, Britain would become a republic. After ten years here, I now know for certain this will never be. Why is that? First of all, Britain doesn't need to. Being a republic won't make her a more democratic state; secondly, the British, rightly or wrongly, are attached to their Royal Family. They don't feel they need to behead its members to feel freer. We did, you don't. Question of temperament.

21

The Way the British Eat

'When I was growing up in England, my idea of a treat was a slice of something called "lardy cake", whose selling point was, in fact, that it was made from lard – that's how bad it was. And we liked it. We knew no better.' Rebecca Mead, journalist

'An army marches on its stomach.' Napoleon

First trip to Britain, age fourteen. Near Southampton. I stayed with a family who insisted I didn't eat with them in the evening and whose twin children called me Aggie. Every morning they gave me my lunch box. Every day for three weeks, I had peanut-butter sandwiches on white bread, an apple, salt-and-vinegar crisps, a can of Fanta and chocolate biscuits. I loved it. Most of my compatriots couldn't stand it, though. After a week, one boy made a reverse-charge call to his mum from a red phone box right in the middle of the countryside: 'Send me proper food, Mum, please!' we could hear him pleading through the door. 'What they give us is too awful. I'm going to die.' The following day a parcel arrived; the boy lived. It reminded me of the scene in Renoir's *Grande Illusion*. In a German prison camp, while German soldiers are fed potatoes and cabbage, French prisoners eat like kings thanks to parcels of foie gras, cognac and *petits pois en gelée* sent every week by one dutiful wealthy family to their imprisoned son.

So was it my fanatical Anglophilia? No, I really did love the contents of my lunch box. A little monotonous perhaps but totally weird, as in from another planet – and weird was good in my book. In the evening, alone in the kitchen of the semi-detached house, I was given greens with gravy, spaghetti or frozen fish and chips; edible but not memorable. What I remember most, apart from feeling slightly unwanted and lonely, was listening to the radio, which, at the time, seemed to play only Wham! hits one after another.

The year after, I asked to go to my beloved exotic England again. This time, I got lucky; I stayed with a wonderful working-class family. They had five children. This time, we could talk and share views about everything and anything. The food they cooked was as strange as could be. Every two days, on the phone to my parents, I'd whisper, finding it difficult to hide my excitement, 'You know what? They boil chicken! No vinaigrette on the salad. They drink tea by the bucket. Mint sauce with overcooked meat. I was genuinely in awe. At the weekend, we had a barbecue in the garden with the neighbours: hamburgers *comme à la maison*, with cardboard-like *petits pains*, the whole thing drowning in ketchup. Divine.

Oh, and I remember the milk. I was fascinated by what looked like *la* national daily delivery; those emblematic round glass bottles appearing magically on everybody's doorstep in the morning. I was soon intrigued by the colour coding of the tops: red, blue, silver and gold. I caught on quickly. My wonderful hosts ordered my favourite, just for me: gold top, the creamier the milk, the better. I swooned with delight at every sip. *Vive l'Angleterre* and English cows!

Newsagents. The first time I entered one, I was looking for a French newspaper. I was fifteen and already passionately interested in politics. As I browsed through the different imported publications, my eye was suddenly caught by the corner of the chocolate display-stand. News could wait. My first step into the world of Cadbury felt like one of the best on-screen love scenes when love at first sight is played out in slow motion to the music of violins. Time stopped. I was a fortress besieged by emotions. Never had I seen so many different types of chocolate bar in my life. I had been the victim of yet another Anglo-Saxon con-spiracy: for fifteen years, everybody had kept this secret from me. Heaven existed after all. Up to then, I hadn't been so sure. Over the three weeks of my stay, I tried them all. I can't remember the names, only the ecstasy. My favourite had to be the same as my older brother's: Maltesers. I'd bring back a suitcase full of them, as they were impossible to find anywhere else but England. And Macleans toothpaste too, for my dad. Don't ask me why. He thought it was the best.

Eight years later, here I was again, back for good. For about a year, I lived my adolescent fantasy of peanut butter, porridge, full-fat milk, clotted cream, scones, biscuits, chocolate bars, crumpets, cheddar, pork pies, bacon and eggs, baked beans, pub lunches with roast beef and Yorkshire pudding, and fish and chips plus the occasional curry. I put on almost a stone. After six months, I came back to Paris for a few days; I had never been away from my home town for so long. Shopping for food at supermarket Monoprix, I ventured first towards the dairy pro-ducts. I stopped and stared and almost cried with wonderment. All those yoghurts, hundreds of different kinds: how could I ever have forgotten? I hadn't realised that for six months, the only yoghurt in my diet had been Petit Filous, the only appealing dairy product in my local Budgens. Browsing through the aisles exhausted me: too much choice. At the cheese counter, I gave up.

I was experiencing the exact same culture shock my British friends had described to me but in reverse. All told me they became aware of how bad food was in England when they first went on holiday abroad, to Greece, Italy, France, Spain or

Portugal. All have a vivid memory of the minute they bit into a fig in Rome, ate a feta and tomato salad in Crete, devoured ham and olives on the Costa del Sol, enjoyed grilled sardines in Provence. As for me, in my fanatical pursuit of becoming British, I had completely forgotten how good and diverse the food was in France. Perhaps my initial approach had been a little too radical.

I didn't need to wait long before striking a balance between my own gastronomic heritage and my newly adopted dietary habits: 1995 heralded the beginning of British modern cuisine. I was saved. It actually turned out as nothing more, nothing less, than a synthesis of Mediterranean gastronomic cultures, with the recurrent trinity of garlic, olive oil and fresh basil.

I wanted to locate the products to cook it myself, though. I got lucky: in supermarkets (I was still struggling to decide which one had the best products and wasn't too expensive), things were changing too. In the bread section, alongside the usual loaves of sliced white and brown bread, and next to the awful *soi-disant* baguettes, Irish, German, Italian, Indian, Middle-Eastern breads started appearing. Foccacia, sour bread, schwarzbrot, nans and pitta. The same happened in other food sections. Devoid of a strong gastronomic tradition, Britain had finally decided to import the best of every culture and make it available to us, the people.

The London restaurant scene also changed. I used to look in guides for good cheap sushi places and Vietnamese canteens. All I found was Wagamama near the British Museum, a strange fusion of Asian noodles, carrot and wheatgrass juice. It took a couple of years and then suddenly a wave of raw fish submerged us all. Even Marks & Spencer started selling sushi lunch boxes to health-obsessed workers. Like most Londoners, I could at last strike a finer balance in my diet.

At home in France, I was never aware of any kind of food but French, except when the family occasionally travelled abroad or when we went to a restaurant: French, Italian, Chinese or Vietnamese. My father was a great cook. He took after his grandmother, who, in occupied France, could knock up a dinner for eight with an egg or two, some flour, a spoonful of fat, a bit of veg and a few herbs from the garden. Invention was at the heart of their cooking. When the fridge seemed empty, he found therein a treasure of goods with which he could whip up a meal in no time. His favourite dishes: *pot au feu*, *petit salé aux lentilles*, *épaule d'agneau*, *riz au lait* and *île flottante*. All have shaped my palate and influenced my taste. On my mother's side, my grandparents also had their specialities. My granddad had a soft tooth and loved waffles and *tarte au riz*, which he made ceremoniously. I was allowed to watch him and was sometimes even allowed the privilege of greasing the dish. As for my grandmother, nobody could match her sorrel soup and *crème anglaise*. All grew their own vegetables, herbs and fruit and traded them with local farmers for eggs or poultry.

Watching Jamie Oliver's TV series about educating young children's taste, I was shocked. First lesson: the young chef shows fresh rhubarb, leeks, courgettes, etc. The children have to guess what they are. A deathly silence meets every question. One boy attempts to answer: 'Potatoes!' he shouts. It was rhubarb. My jaw dropped in disbelief. Hang on, I'm a city-dweller, never lived in the countryside and am really bad at naming plants and animals (to the dismay of my family), but, hey, how can one be so alienated from nature as not to know what a potato looks like? Despite incessant talks of a crisis in French gastronomy, I truly believe such a scene would be impossible there, as we have been taught to take an interest in what we eat and care about its origin from a very early age.

Here lies the crux of the matter: there is not a single French family who doesn't have ties with the country and the farming community. Agriculture and *le terroir*[1] are crucially important in

1. A word that is difficult to translate as it conveys an abstract sense of belonging to a particular region of France and its culture.

France. French politicians have always fought hard to help preserve a strong agricultural industry, via heavy subsidies if necessary. These rural roots have something almost mythological about them, and they influence what we really want on our plate. As long as the French care about what they eat, French farmers will constitute a strong lobby.

Seen from France, British agriculture seems to have gone to the dogs, yet another victim of the all-mighty market. Maybe because the British, after all, don't seem to mind so much what they eat. As a result, most of the products one eats in the UK are imported. The few remaining farmers have been given the responsibility to keep the British countryside pretty for when city-dwellers visit. Sure, there are still a few British farmers who sell their wonderful products at, say, Borough Market at London Bridge, but such quality is only available to the rich. So what's the use if *le peuple* cannot benefit from *sa terre*? What Britain needs is a better standard of ordinary produce that is available and affordable to all. That would be truly revolutionary.

The whole debate about food in France actually revolves around one idea, one key notion, that of authenticity. There is almost an unwritten law that prevents you from going to, say, a Tex-Mex restaurant in Rome where the cook is German. Why? Because it just doesn't make sense. You must eat Italian in Italy, French in France and so forth. There can be exceptions but only if based on authenticity. You may go to an Italian restaurant in Paris only if you know for certain that the owner and chef are Italian and that the cooking is done with Italian products. Otherwise, it's fake, therefore worthless. There are rules and traditions. Always be wary of a *crêperie* whose menu advertises smoked salmon and cream-cheese *galettes*. A *galette* is not a bagel. It just cannot be done. Rigid doctrine for sure, but at least you always know where you stand in the shadowy world of *galettes*. And this goes for all facets of French gastronomy. You may transcend the rules, but if you do, you'd better be bloody good at it, i.e. be an artist. French chefs know the rules; can therefore break them and create new ones; they are artists and are therefore accepted with respect.

Needless to say, I went in pursuit of authentic English cooking. And I found it. Initially, in the first gastro-pubs to see daylight, in early 1996. They served deliciously hearty food like treacle tart and spotted dick. Thick, hot puddings admirably suited to the damp weather. Then, I couldn't resist treating myself to restaurants such as Rules, or the £15 three-course Sunday brunch at the Ivy. I wanted to know about game, Irish oysters, Stilton. Were they really that good? Yes, they were. I could at last tell the folks back home that actually we had got it all wrong: British food can be tasty. I also wandered through London in search of superlative fish and chips. My methodological research took me from the East End to Pimlico and from Peckham to Golders Green. There was no end to my curiosity. Every time I travelled somewhere in the UK, I had to try the local speciality: clotted cream and scones in St Ives in Cornwall, seafood in coastal towns, sole in Dover, venison sausages in Cumberland, haggis in Edinburgh, etc. Fed up to the back teeth with Marks & Spencer's Cheddar, I discovered there was actually more to British cheese. The Neal's Yard shops provided the divinely pungent products suitable for a cheese-lover. The Stinking Bishop became a favourite long before Wallace and Gromit adopted it.

Wine, ah yes, wine. I still occasionally wince when reading a wine list in a restaurant in the UK. Let's face it, New World wine has superseded French wine in the British affections. I'm not apportioning blame, because I myself can never find a decent bottle of French wine in the supermarkets of London. I have the feeling the British suddenly had enough of French producers who, for years, exported their worst wines thinking it was good enough for the British. Tasteless plonk like le Piat d'Or, never drunk by the French, a product purely for exportation. Their condescension only brought them ruin. In the 1990s, more and more British consumers turned to less pretentious and less complex wines. New World wines are strong, relatively reliable in quality and not overly expensive. They may lack personality and depth and be unsurprising, but for that price why should one care?

Today, my diet mirrors both my life as a Londoner and my Parisian education; it is multicultural in essence but above all true to its origins (with the occasional regressive Cadbury craving, to which I yield willingly).

22

Frangleterre

There was once a man with a vision. He was Guy Mollet, President of the Council of the 4th Republic, the French Prime Minister of the time. On 10 September 1956, he proposed to the British, by which I mean he suggested to his counterpart, Anthony Eden, that France and Britain unite and merge into one country. The BBC's Mike Thompson unearthed what had been a highly confidential correspondence at the National Archives in early 2007 and showed it to my old professor at the Sorbonne, Henri Soutou, who started choking in disbelief at the news, live on Radio 4.

When the BBC called me with an invitation to a breakfast programme to discuss Mollet's proposal, I thought, *non, ce n'est pas possible*: this must be a joke. I phoned the corporation's switchboard to check whether the producer who had contacted me really worked there. She did. Still thinking I was the victim of a practical joke, I sent nervous emails to British colleagues working in daily news (surely they would know about it). Have you heard? I asked anxiously. Gradually, the picture emerged: it was all true. However, the 'worst' was yet to come. Totally unfazed at having been rebuffed by his friend Anthony, and not taking no for an answer, Guy proposed again, exactly two weeks later, down on one knee: would Britain take France into the Commonwealth? he asked boldly, adding immediately that it wouldn't be 'such a problem' for the

Republican French to accept being ruled by Her Majesty the Queen.

Quoi! I was the one to choke this time. How did the French Premier dare? No, of course it wouldn't be such a problem being ruled by the queen, if we could give her a taste of our sweet G, *la guillotine*! But perhaps that was the plan. Oh, I see, good one, Guy: what we couldn't do in 1815, we'd do in 1956. Didn't we owe our admirable British friends a big favour for having saved our skin in 1940–1945? We should infiltrate and strike: pretend we're one country and, voilà, from one masterly stroke of the blade, erase the Royal Family.

But no, that wasn't the plan: Guy was serious. He had been an English teacher before the war, and his years in the Resistance made him an impenitent Anglophile. He did want the two countries to become one.

Though the bride looked decidedly seductive, Anthony Eden and his cabinet turned her down. Britain would not marry France. It was only twelve years since Laurence Olivier had directed his masterpiece *Henry V*, but the echo of King Henry of England whispering sweet words in Catherine of France's ears had faded from Britain's memory. There was no more witchcraft on France's lips.

At least Eden's decision came quickly; France would not agonise over her lover's indecision. To British ears, the idea sounded indeed mad beyond belief. However, if the British cabinet had looked at it more closely, they would have realised how visionary the French proposal was; in truth, it seemed the only way forward for the two former world powers. But British politicians were still full of memories from the war, still bitter at France's lamentable let-down in 1940. The paradox of course was that Britain loved her more than they did anybody else; after all, twice in twenty years they had sent the country's youth to die for France on her shores. The British cabinet were just weary and wary of France's true intentions, and America felt like a less complicated ally, if rather dull. Besides, British pragmatists do neither vision nor revolution. And Mollet's proposal was just that: revolutionary and visionary.

In October 1956, Britain fatefully chose the US over France and Europe, even though the Suez crisis in which they were both embroiled should have taught Britain, as it did France, that in order to counterbalance the American and Russian bullies Europe needed to be one, united and strong.

Just six weeks later, on 6 November 1956, the day after the USSR and the USA sent an ultimatum to Britain and France to withdraw from Egypt, cheeky France turned to German Chancellor Konrad Adenauer. Another proposal. This time, the groom said *ja*! France and Germany agreed to lay the foundations of the future European Union: it was the beginning of a beautiful friendship.

However, the romantic in me can't help but sigh: if only Britain had said *oui* to France.

23

Humour

At last, I know what defines Britishness. The months of national soul-searching led by Gordon Brown may now stop. The chancellor can relax – I have cracked it.

So what constitutes Britishness? Not tolerance, which too often verges on blindness. Not the three Bs, bacon, bingo and booze, though they certainly make the top 10. Not decency and fairness, which nevertheless emerge, magnificently, in difficult circumstances. Not even resilience, which comes a good second. It is humour. Funny you never thought of that. Fools. Guarding a treasure, oblivious.

The existential question has always been: why were the British made funnier than anybody else on earth? This is clearly a blatant case of discrimination on which the European Court of Justice should legislate. Such injustice usually leaves Americans goggle-eyed, mouth agape, and has for centuries stoked anger in the egalitarian hearts of the French. Never wondered why Joan of Arc flared up each time she saw a Brit? And what do you think really lay beneath Napoleon's incandescence? Lust, yes, but, more importantly, envy. Envy for this otherworldly gift, Monty Python's Holy Grail, something neither of them ever had: humour.

Think I'm talking nonsense? Here is proof: humour is the only topic taken seriously in Britain, the universal sauce that makes thoughts or ideas palatable. In Britain, safer to leave one's umbrella at home than one's humour. Never wondered why Tony Blair got elected three times? Surely not for his Labourless manifesto. No. It is because when the guy is up against the wall he can crack a joke about his wife and his next-door neighbour and get the world laughing – at Gordon's expense. Can't help but admire him. There are two sorts of people in Britain, the bores and the funny ones: the Browns and the Blairs. In France, each time Mitterrand made a joke, somebody died; today, each time Chirac pulls somebody's leg, the CAC40 takes a plunge at the Paris stock exchange.

British humour is the Enigma code we foreigners never manage to break. What could be the ingredients of this sauce the recipe of which we can never master? The social hypocrisy rife at the very heart of Britain, which has always offered one of the best sources of British humour. Laughter and irony sparkle in each Brit as their insides and outsides clash against one another.

British humour also derives from the nation's taste for playing – games, sport, anything – and for loving the performance of banter down the pub. Everything's an excuse to laugh. Take a look at Parliament. This is surely the best comedy theatre the world has ever known. From (William) Hogarth to (Simon) Hoggart, its interpreters *de choix*, it can hold the entire world transfixed. I would suggest that the *légion d'honneur* be bestowed upon Hoggart for having written, among other memorable lines: 'Mr Oaten is always billed as the "toughest" Liberal Democrat, which is like being the country's tallest dwarf. Or its most combative hamster.'

What would the British do without a sense of humour? It's the best survival kit in a country where 'power shower' is an oxymoron that stands for everything that doesn't work. And better be armed with a strong sense of derision in a country where one calls monarchy democracy, and where the Royal Family can only really be tolerated if treated as some kind of elaborate high-class joke.

So, what to do with this great unappreciated treasure at the heart of Britain? First, part ways with the humourless neo-cons of the USA and meet the challenge born of the so-called clash of civilisations with the best of British humour: abandon the laughably named War on Terror for a War on Witlessness. Take down today's fanatics, who cannot laugh at themselves, with your own Weapons of Mass Derision.

Jacques Tati may have had the style and sophistication, an abstract sense of humour, but I doubt he's ever made your sides split. As for the American Hardy, he surely proved no match for the Englishman Laurel. So the British have it. Except, that is, for one who beats them all: Jerry Lewis.

Just kidding.

Conclusion

I don't think there will ever be a satisfying conclusion to Anglo-French relations; the eternal bickering and passionate making up.

Nature might one day provide *la solution*. It is said that, each year, the British Isles move southwards. When we can walk directly from Brittany to Devon and from Picardie to Kent, then perhaps, *l'entente* will become *totale*.

In the meantime, let's keep up the jousting, cordially. *Touché*!